The Jeffersonian
Tradition

The Jeffersonian Tradition

Brion McClanahan

THE JEFFERSONIAN TRADITION
Copyright © 2021 by Brion McClanahan

ALL RIGHTS RESERVED. No part of this publication may be reproduced, distributed, or transmitted in any form or by any means, including photocopying, recording, or other electronic or mechanical methods, or by any information storage and retrieval system without the prior written permission of the publisher, except in the case of very brief quotations embodied in critical reviews and certain other non-commercial uses permitted by copyright law.

Red Mill Publishing

PO Box 3761

Auburn, AL 36831

ISBN: 978-1-7349504-1-0

10 9 8 7 6 5 4 3 2 1

Table of Contents

Part I: The Jeffersonian Tradition

We Are All Jeffersonians 1

Jefferson's Rightful Remedy. 5

Rethinking the Declaration of Independence. 9

We Need No Declaration Of Independence .13

"Liberty Ought To Be The Direct End Of Your Government" 17

The United States Is (Are) Not A Nation! 21

Why the Tenth Amendment? 25

Decentralization for Socialists: A Brief Primer. 29

Let's Give Up on the (Unwritten) Constitution. 33

Our Conservative Constitution. 37

Who's Supreme: The Supremacy Clause Smackdown 43

Rewriting History: A Response to Ian Millhiser's Diatribe on "Tentherism." 49

A Neo-Impressionist Jefferson Portrait 59

Amendment IX 61

The Articles of Confederation. 63

Judicial Power: The Founders' Design 67

Cheesehead Secessionists. 71

National Democratic Party (NDP). 73

Part II: Lincolnites, Neoconservatives, and Progressives

Democracy, Liberty, Equality: Lincoln's American Revolution 81

All Hail Abe! 89

Mt. Rushmore Myth 91

Solidifying the Cult of Lincoln, Pennywise 95

Lincolnites are Crazed Warmongers 99

Republican Tyranny 103

Apostles of Racism 107

What Would Lincoln Do? 111

A Lonely Opposition 115

The Five Most Underrated Presidents 119

The Five Most Overrated Presidents 121

Establishment Historians' Presidents 125

King Barack 129

Obama and the Prize 133

Vote Obama! The Robert W. Whitaker Effect 135

Was the Civil War [sic] Necessary? 139

The American Tradition is Anti-War 145

Hamiltonian Nationalism 149

Hamilton: Liar 153

Part III: Southern Comfort

Please "Dump Dixie" 159

Clyde N. Wilson 163

Southern Conservatism and the "Gilded Age" 167

People Along the Way: Dan Smoot 175

Jefferson Davis and the Lame Lion of Lynchburg. 179

The Tuckers of Virginia 183

Fire Cured Dark Leaf 187

Confederate Coca-Cola 191

A Black Armband for Southern Education 195

Jefferson Davis and the Kenner Mission 199

The Slaveholders' Dilemma 201

Twitter Historians Distort History, Again 203

"Daniel Boone Was A Man". 209

Sunnyside and Sleepy Hollow 211

Calhoun's Definition of Conservative. 213

Conservative as "Defender of Liberty". 215

Catalonia and the Southern Tradition 219

Pope Francis and the Southern Tradition 223

Part I:
The Jeffersonian Tradition

We Are All Jeffersonians

THOMAS JEFFERSON IS PERHAPS THE GREATEST ENIGMA of the American age. He wrote and spoke on so many topics that he has become the symbol of virtually every strain of uniquely American political thought. Jefferson is the democrat, the agrarian, the federalist, the republican, the radical, the conservative, the statesman, the planter, the intellectual, the philosopher, the educator. Volumes have been written on his life and legacy, and yet we still search for the man. More will be written, but somehow his name will remain both predictable and elusive, like the bite of the first frost, the first bud of spring, the first warm Southern summer day. We know it is there and that it will come, but when is always a mystery. Jefferson is the crackling log and a warm hearth on a cold day, the reliable anchor to our ship of state. We know him because he is us. Even now, as many Americans attempt to demonize and jettison his name and legacy, to reduce him to little more than a vicious slave holder with a cunning and vindictive stripe, Jefferson has currency in our age, if we choose to listen.

Next to Washington, he is the most American of the founding generation, and his name defined a later generation of Americans. Long before the Age of Jackson, there was the Age of Jefferson, the boundless and restless American foray into the great frontier, peopled by farmers and a hearty individualism that became the hallmark of the American experience. Jefferson embraced it like no other, and in contrast to Jackson, Jefferson knew how to articulate a vision. Jackson rode Jefferson's coattails, reacted to, and then rejected Jefferson's American man, the free thinker, the independent spirit, the American statesman guided by a brand of republicanism that was purely American.

Part I: The Jeffersonian Tradition

If Jefferson bequeathed anything to America, it is not the proposition that "all men are created equal." Equality under the law had been an accepted maxim long before Jefferson wrote that line in the Declaration of Independence. No, Jefferson's gift to America is found in the last paragraph of the Declaration, the firm commitment to a federal republic of "Free and Independent States" comprised of the people who made each community unique. This is Jefferson as the conservative.

Jefferson believed that States were organic communities built on a common culture. He could be a radical within his own community, but it ended there. Whereas Jefferson had a grand vision for the "Empire of Liberty," that was only in relation to the idea of independence. It was not a "city upon a hill" sermon of subjugation. Jefferson, in his "flatteries of hope" thought the "ball of liberty" would one day "roll around the globe" and as he wrote to John Dickinson in 1801, Jefferson believed that, "A just and solid republican government maintained here will be a standing monument and example for the aim and imitation of the people of other countries; and I join… in the hope and belief that they will see from our example that a free government is of all others the most energetic; that the inquiry which has been excited among the mass of mankind by our revolution and its consequences will ameliorate the condition of man over a great portion of the globe." Yet, he was under no illusion that such would be easy or in every case desirable. He did not think republicanism would take hold in South America nor did he think that everyone the world over would embrace liberty. It was the American condition, and maybe only the Virginian condition, which is why he wanted Southerners to avoid the "dark Federalist mills of the North." If so, Jefferson would defend it in his own country to the last.

His dedication to the American order is evident in his various statements on political philosophy. His grand statements on federalism and "nullification" in the Kentucky Resolutions are consistent with a belief in the necessity of community and the people as the safeguard of liberty. He wrote in 1809 that, "The people of every country are the only safe guardians of their own rights and are the only instruments which can be used for their destruction. And certainly, they would never consent to be so used were they not deceived. To avoid this, they should be instructed to a certain degree." The Sedition Act was not only unconstitutional, but it also violated the ordered liberty of Virginia, and was an attempt by a foreign power (New England) to impose its will on another people. Jefferson the philosopher rejected such cultural imperialism, just as he rejected the cultural imperialism of Great Britain in 1776. He later said that the Declaration was not a radical pronouncement of new rights but simply the articulation of the American mind. In Jefferson's case that mind was forged in the hardwood covered hills of Virginia.

Jefferson's Northwest Ordinance and his support for political independence provide ample evidence that his "democracy" was rooted in the culture of a people and the voice of a place. When each territory in the old Northwest reached five thousand free male inhabitants, it could form a government, with a representative ratio of 500 to 1. Such a government would be responsive to the community and the culture that created it. It would be democratic in its purest form. In contrast to a "national democracy," this type of democracy could be controlled from within by neighbors in a republican experiment. Once the territory reached sixty thousand free inhabitants, it could be admitted to the Union as a State "on equal footing with the existing States." The people would then form a constitution and a republican form of government, but such States and the government thereof would be the expression of the political community and not of the Union as a whole. As in Virginia, the constitutions of these new States would be formed by the culture of the people who resided therein.

Jefferson later said that the political culture of each new State may in time sever its ties to the old American Union. That was perfectly reasonable, logical, and ultimately preferable. He had his own reason to worry about a Union of incompatible things. The "fire bell in the night" Jefferson famously warned against was not a fear over eradication of slavery per se, but over the potential cultural imperialism of the North and the destruction of true federalism. If States could be coerced by a numerical majority, then the culture of each would be ground into grist by alien peoples and alien agendas. Jefferson did not want other political communities to fall prey to this type of political suicide. Separation would be preferable to cultural destruction.

That alone made Jefferson a conservative. He could wax philosophical about changing the culture of his own backyard, and many of his contemporaries viewed his political theories as radical departures from the status quo, but Jefferson never sought to apply those theories to Massachusetts or Pennsylvania. He was a cosmopolitan thinker knee deep in Virginia soil and eye level with his mountains. Modern Americans should learn from such a vision. He would sweep his own backdoor but leave it to someone else to sweep theirs. Jefferson's federalism is the American vision of political unity, a unity that was only perverted by the social engineers, do-gooders, and reformers intent on remaking the rest of the world in their image. Jefferson was not this type of activist, nor did he possess the Puritanical crusading zeal of New England.

His America held for more than eighty years, and even after a brutal war that claimed the lives of a million men, there were those, North and South, who formed a truly national vision of the American spirit. These Jeffersonians still exist, principally in the small towns and rural pockets of the American landscape.

The South has remained dedicated to Jefferson's vision longer than anywhere else. Its small farms and main streets have only recently been occupied by Wall Street corporations, big banks, and cultural Marxists. If anywhere should lead a Jeffersonian renaissance in America, it is the South. Federalism is catching fire in America again. Jefferson's name, so long vilified by the modern left, is echoing in American political chambers. The slumbering spirit of American self-government has found its voice, if only a whisper now. It can and will eventually roar. Jefferson will have the final say, and we may finally understand who he was and who he is.

Jefferson's Rightful Remedy

VICTOR DAVIS HANSON has a strange and misguided infatuation with "Confederates." In June, his widely read *National Review* piece on the Confederate Battle Flag equated the Confederacy to a "racist separatist group" like Benito Mussolini's fascist Italy, and just this week, Hanson suggested that so-called "sanctuary cities" are the new "Confederates."

Hanson's overarching argument in both, and for that matter in much of his political treatises, is that "lawlessness"—which he defines as any threat to the political class or ruling order—undermines good government. To Hanson, there is no better example of lawlessness in America than the doctrines of state interposition (nullification) and secession.

Hanson is a very good military historian, perhaps one of the best in the modern era, but his understanding of the foundations of American government, the original principles of the "Union," and for that matter a firm grasp of eighteenth and nineteenth century American political history, lacks cogency. He often relies on half-truths and straw man arguments to prop up his claims.

For example, Hanson suggested that John C. Calhoun "declared…that federal tariffs should not apply to his state." False. Calhoun and South Carolina, through a popularly elected convention of the people in 1832, insisted that the protective tariffs passed by Congress and signed by Presidents John Quincy Adams and Andrew Jackson between 1828 and 1832 were unconstitutional because they violated the "general welfare" of the Union and the uniform distribution of taxes among the States. They unequally benefitted one section (the North) and burdened the other (the South). Neither Calhoun nor the people of South Carolina said that *all* tariffs did not apply to South Carolina, only unconstitutional tariffs like the 1828 Tariff of Abominations and its successors. In fact, after the tariff was reduced, South Carolina rescinded its Ordinance of Nullification and began collecting the tariff.

He then suggests that nullification is the "illiberal pedigree" of the Confederacy. False again. Nullification was used *before* the American War for Independence to resist unconstitutional acts by the British Parliament. The famous Suffolk Resolves of 1774 (from Massachusetts) declared that, "That no obedience is due from this province to either or any part of the acts above-mentioned [Intolerable Acts], but that they be rejected as the attempts of a wicked administration to enslave America." Further, the Resolves urged all Massachusetts law enforcement officials to "refuse to carry into execution the orders" of the now illegal courts of Massachusetts. That is nullification. The First Continental Congress later adopted a modified version of the Resolves.

Of course, the British would call this lawlessness, as they did the first American war of secession. The founding generation considered the "rights of Englishmen" to be paramount to supposedly supreme but unconstitutional and illegal acts of Parliament. The British also argued that the American War for Independence was little more than a cover for the protection of slavery. Good thing the Limeys across the pond did not get to write our history books or Hanson would be forced to conclude that the Stars and Stripes represents a "racist separatist group."

His contempt for nullification also ignores that when the Constitution was ratified in 1788, *proponents* of the document swore that should the general government exceed its delegated authority, the States, as Roger Sherman of Connecticut said, would be "powerful enough to check it." How so was the question. The Tenth Amendment offered the solution. Notice Sherman did not say the federal courts would be powerful enough to check it, but the States.

Nullification was first introduced as an actionable doctrine by Thomas Jefferson and James Madison in 1798 through the Virginia and Kentucky Resolutions. They targeted the illegal and infamous Sedition Act of 1798, a law that any clear-thinking person both then and now could see violated both the First and Tenth Amendments. I would surmise that both Jefferson and Madison knew something about the nature of the Union and American government.

That said, Hanson is correct that "sanctuary cities" are illegal. The Constitution delegates the authority to set "uniform rules for naturalization" to the Congress in Article 1, Section 8. A State or a city cannot ignore a *constitutional* law, only *unconstitutional* acts. Federal immigration law is not unconstitutional and thus should be enforced.

The same cannot be said for "marriage equality." The Constitution does not grant the general government any authority over marriage. That has long been strictly a State issue. The federal courts have overstepped their boundaries, and thus Kim Davis followed the correct *constitutional* path in ignoring an unconstitutional federal ruling. Hanson incorrectly claims that sanctuary cities and Kim Davis are two sides of the same coin. Far from it.

Federalism and the original Constitution are on the ropes (if they are not already knocked out) in the American polity, and as conservatives we need to be consistent in our application of the original principles of American government. Rand Paul was correct in the last presidential debate that so many of our so-called "conservative" minds have adopted policies and taken positions on a variety of issues that violate the original Constitution they so stridently say they defend.

Much of the legislation passed by Congress today would never have been considered constitutional by the founding generation. History has given us clues as to what would be their response. Jefferson called it the "rightful" remedy. We call it nullification.

It is neither lawless nor illegal, but a proper defense of the "ancient constitutions of our fathers" and the "rights of Englishmen" passed down to Americans. The author of the Suffolk Resolves, Joseph Warren, said, "That it is an indispensable duty which we owe to God, our country, ourselves and posterity, by all lawful ways and means in our power to maintain, defend and preserve those civil and religious rights and liberties, for which many of our fathers fought, bled and died, and to hand them down entire to future generations." We are their posterity, and we should heed his call.

Rethinking the Declaration of Independence

THOMAS JEFFERSON WROTE in 1825 that he intended the Declaration of Independence to be "an expression of the American mind, and to give to that expression the proper tone and spirit called for by the occasion." Yet, he did not propose the Declaration should "find out new principles, or new arguments, never before thought of...." The last statement is the clearest articulation of what Jefferson and other members of the founding generation thought of the Declaration. It was a restatement of the rights of Englishmen, modeled in large part by previous works of English and American law. The Declaration was not a radical document or a deviation from accepted constitutional norms, as the famous historian Gordon Wood suggests. But the idea that Jefferson and other founders would be modern liberals persists, and that is why Barack Obama can argue with a straight face that he is following the founding documents of the United States. Such thinking needs a "radical" correction and a better understanding of the Declaration is the key.

In 1100, King Henry I of England agreed to restrictions on his power through the Charter of Liberties. The English barons rejected absolute authority and sought to preserve traditional decentralized "government." Just over one hundred years later, King John was forced again by the English nobles to sign the Magna Charta. The "Great Charter," as it is known in English, declared that the king was not above the law—making him essentially equal to the nobles—and it resisted the trend toward centralization in England. Though on the books, the Magna Charta was often ignored by more powerful English monarchs, but several of its provisions became the basis of English common law, most notably the writ of *habeas corpus*.

When England erupted in civil war in the seventeenth century, the Parliament asserted its authority, and by 1688 had become the driving force behind English law and policy. When King James II was expelled from England in 1688, the Parliament forced the incoming monarch, William of Orange, to sign the English Bill of Rights. It condemned James II for violating the rights of Englishmen, what the Parliament called the "laws and liberties of this kingdom," and placed restrictions on the powers of the monarch. Jefferson essentially copied the form of the English Bill of Rights in writing the Declaration. Thus, Jefferson's indictment of King George III was not a radical departure from accepted English practices. He was following English tradition, which in turn he adapted to American circumstances. This formed the American tradition, a conservative rather than radical tradition.

Additionally, Jefferson borrowed language from George Mason's Virginia Declaration of Resolves in drafting the Declaration. Mason asserted that "all men are by nature equally free and independent, and have certain inherent rights…namely the enjoyment of life and liberty, with the means of acquiring and possessing property, and pursuing and maintaining happiness and safety." Jefferson altered this in his original draft to "We hold these truths to be sacred and undeniable: that all men are created equal; that they are endowed by their creator with inherent and inalienable rights; that among these are life, liberty, and the pursuit of happiness." By "equal," Jefferson meant that all citizens or freeholders are, as Mason wrote, born "equally free and independent" under the law. The barons of England asserted their legal equality with the king in 1100 and 1215. Jefferson was not stating anything new. And Jefferson simply shortened Mason's language—which he borrowed from John Locke's 1689 publication Two Treatises on Civil Government¬—to "life, liberty, and the pursuit of happiness." Everyone understood that Jefferson equated "happiness" with property and safety.

Another famous historian, Joseph Ellis, contends that Jefferson viewed government as an "alien force." But Jefferson never used that term. He argued that the colonists had suffered patiently under "a long train of abuses and usurpations" and an "absolute Despotism." Thus, it was their "right" and "duty, to throw off such Government and to provide new Guards for their future security." This had been done countless times in human history, and as recently as 1689 in England. Jefferson did not think the English system of government was tyrannical, and in particular did not denounce Virginia colonial government. Only the "present King of Great Britain," George III, deserved condemnation. Government had an obligation, in his words, to protect the "safety and happiness" of the people. That is not an anti-government view, but of course, Jefferson believed there should be limits on government power and, most importantly, the size and scope of government.

The Declaration of Independence did not "create" the "United States." Jefferson called it the "united States," or simply the States united. Virginia and Maryland both separately declared their independence from Great Britain, with Virginia doing so over a month before the Declaration was ratified in the Continental Congress. The colonies became "FREE AND INDEPENDENT STATES." Jefferson made a conscious decision to choose the word State. A State, in the 18th century, was a sovereign political entity. In the same document, Jefferson called Great Britain a "State." Thus, Virginia, Massachusetts, New York, or any other American State, were equal to the mother country. They were not shires, parishes, counties, or provinces subservient to a "united States" government. The Declaration, then, is a decentralizing document, and the first governing document of the United States, the Articles of Confederation, reaffirmed that fact.

Most people mistake centralization as a "conservative" tendency. Human history proves otherwise. Centralization, whether political, cultural, or religious, does not conserve anything but the imperial traits of the centralizers, whether Marxists, theocratic zealots, or something else. Religions, cultures, customs, conventions, constitutions, economies, etc. are often ruined by the centralizers, and thus, centralization is always a "progressive" trend, not a conservative one, and typically the reaction to centralization is a conservative reaction, a push to preserve the culture, customs, or traditions of a particular people or place. Likewise, all empires have broken under the strain of conservative resistance to the imperial order. Jefferson and the men of the founding generation declared their independence to preserve English liberties. It was a decentralized, conservative movement.

Thinking of the Declaration and the War for Independence this way sheds light on who Americans are as a people. They are a naturally conservative group who love liberty and who are also inclined to preserve the traditions, customs, and cultures of their communities and families. Most men in the founding generation viewed "provincialism" as a badge of honor. They were Virginians, New Yorkers, Pennsylvanians, Massachusettians, and Marylanders first and foremost and Americans second. They defended the rights of their sister States, but did not want another State, foreign or domestic, interfering in the concerns of their local community. In the rush to force "our" will on other Americans (or on the world), we forget this lesson. The American tradition, as exemplified by the Declaration of Independence and the founding generation, favors limited, decentralized government that has as its only charge the protection of life, liberty, and property, and the maintenance of the cultures, customs, conventions, and constitutions of the States and local communities. The Declaration did not "create" new rights, it simply re-affirmed the old, and it is America's conservative document.

We Need No Declaration Of Independence

MANY CURRENT AMERICANS, indeed perhaps most, regard the firing on Fort Sumter in April 1861 as a premeditated act of violence by South Carolina against the United States Government. They further assume that violence was both intended and desired by Southern leaders in the months leading to the War Between the States. After all, the South should have known that a bloody conflict would follow secession. Such a revolutionary act had to be met with force. This is a misconception and a gross distortion of the public record. Southern men anticipated that violence might be a possibility, but they hoped not a probability, not out of weakness, but because they considered the act of secession to be a perfectly legal, defensible, logical, and most importantly, American option in 1860 and 1861.

Jefferson Davis articulated this point in his First Inaugural Address, but he was not alone. Across the South, delegates to State secession conventions consistently spoke of peace and the legal and philosophical underpinnings of secession. This was no revolutionary act. In November 1860 during the legislative session to consider calling a secession convention in Georgia, Robert Toombs insisted, "We need no declaration of independence." Why? Because "Above eighty-four years ago our fathers won that by the sword from Great Britain, and above seventy years ago Georgia, with the twelve other confederates, as free, sovereign, and independent States, having perfect governments already in existence, for purposes and objects clearly expressed, and with powers clearly defined, erected a common agent for the attainment of these purposes by the exercise of those powers, and called this agent the United States of America."

The phrase "free, sovereign, and independent States" became a major point of reference across the South. It could not be denied that in 1776 the States, acting as free and independent political entities, separately declared their independence from Great Britain, though Joseph Story attempted to do so in his famous *Commentaries*. The several attempts at Northern secession in the years before 1860 underlined this position. How could members of the founding generation, several of whom served in both the Philadelphia Convention of 1787 and their respective State ratifying conventions, advance such a "radical" idea? Because secession was inherent in the adoption of the Constitution.

Ratification by the people of the States did not bind the State to support unconstitutional legislation or coercion by the general government, nor did it abridge the sovereignty of the States. Only a sovereign entity could delegate or grant a power, as all powers are in the Constitution, and as proponents of the Constitution consistently emphasized, the Constitution was a compact "between the States so ratifying the same." They also maintained that the States could never be coerced by the central authority. The people of the States were acceding to a Constitution as a sovereign act by their State. By default, then, the people could secede from the same instrument. This was not denied for most of early American history, and by 1860 Southern leaders did not think anything had changed.

For example, during the Alabama Secession Convention, Governor A.B. Moore argued:

> Should Alabama secede from the Union, as I think she ought, the responsibility, in the eyes of all just men, will not rest upon her, but upon those who have driven her in self-defence, to assume that position. Has Alabama the right peacefully to withdraw from the Union, without subjecting herself to any rightful authority of the Federal Government to coerce her into the Union? Of her right to do so, I have no doubt. She is a Sovereign State, and retains every right and power not delegated to the Federal Government in the written Constitution. That Government has no powers, except such as are delegated in the Constitution, or such as are necessary to carry these powers into execution. The Federal Government was established for the protection, and not for destruction or injury of Constitutional rights. A Sovereign State has a right to judge of the wrongs or injuries that may be done her, and to determine upon the mode and measures of redress.... If Alabama should withdraw from the Union, she would not be guilty of treason, even if a Sovereign State could commit treason. The Constitution says: "Treason against the

United States shall consist only in levying war against them, or in adhering to their enemies, giving them aid and comfort." The Federal Government has the right to use its military power "to execute the laws of the Union, surpress insurrections, and repel invasions." If a State withdraws from the Union, the Federal Government has no power, under the Constitution, to use the military force against her, for there is no law to enforce the submission of a sovereign State, nor would such a withdrawal be either an insurrection or an invasion.

Later in the Convention, delegate Lewis M. Stone, in considering a resolution to offer aid to South Carolina should the United States attempt force compel her to remain in the Union, contended that:

> All the powers of the State of Alabama should be pledged to aid in resisting any attempt to coerce a seceding State back into the Union. Sir, the Southern States recognize the right of secession. It constitutes the very essence of State sovereignty, and is inseparable from it. A State is the best and sole judge of her own grievances, and as a party to the Federal compact must, herself, decide in the last resort "as well of the infraction as of the mode and measure of redress." If, in her sovereign capacity, she determines to resume her independence, can we, who have a common interest in the protection of this right, look calmly on and see her invaded by Federal soldiers? Sir, the Convention which framed our Constitution expressly refused to grant to the General Government the power to employ force against a State. The States came into the Union "free, sovereign and independent." They have never parted with their freedom or sovereignty. They established a Government to act as their agent; and now, to permit that agent to employ force against the States would be to sanction the grossest usurpation. It would be converting the Government into a despotism. Sir, the Union was never intended to be preserved by force. The fact that the power to employ force against a State was refused in the Convention which framed the Constitution, proves that those who constructed our Government knew that it could not be maintained by force. Of what value would the Union be, if the States composing it had to be reduced to obedience by the strong arm of military power? The permanence and security of our Government depend alone

upon the principle of common affection and common interest. Force is the last argument of kings, and cannot keep these States together.

Abraham Lincoln thought otherwise, and the Republican Party, many of whom had supported the secession of New England just over a decade before, sustained Lincoln's path to war. This is the great tragedy of the event. Secession itself is a peaceful act of self-determination. Lincoln's resolve to "enforce the laws" mirrored that of George III in 1774 and 1775. As Patrick Henry asked in 1775, "Are fleets and armies necessary to a work of love and reconciliation? Have we shown ourselves so unwilling to be reconciled that force must be called in to win back our love? Let us not deceive ourselves, sir. These are the implements of war and subjugation; the last arguments to which kings resort. I ask gentlemen, sir, what means this martial array, if its purpose be not to force us to submission?"

If Lincoln firmly believed in self-government, in a government "of the people, by the people, and for the people," then the Southern States would have been allowed to go in peace and the deaths of over 1,000,000 men would have been avoided. It can only be hoped that the peaceful wave of secession movements that have risen in Europe and elsewhere in the last twenty years has blunted the blade of coercion, particularly in the land that made the act popular in the modern era, first in 1776 and then again in 1860 and 1861.

"Liberty Ought To Be The Direct End Of Your Government"

ONE OF THE GREATEST AMERICAN STATESMEN, Patrick Henry, was born on this day (May 29) in 1736. Jefferson once said that Henry single-handedly delivered Virginia to the cause of independence. He also said that Henry was the laziest reader he knew, and modern critics consider Henry to have been nothing more than a sliver-tongued, hayseed demagogue. Certainly, he did not have a stellar education, and his acumen as a merchant and farmer were suspect at best. But Henry had a gift for oratory, and he maximized his talent, first as an attorney, then as a young firebrand member of the Virginia House of Burgesses, and later as a leader in Virginia politics, both during and after the American War for Independence. Jefferson was, in fact, jealous of Henry's gift of public persuasion. Most were. Henry did not always win the debate, and he often took great risks to protect Virginians from all types of schemes, particularly those which originated in government. He called his stand against power manly. We should, too.

Henry considered the ancient liberties of Englishmen, the traditions of their fathers, codified by blood, steel, and vigilance over generations, to be the pillars upon which good government rested. His famous speech at St. John's Church in Richmond in 1775 was more than a call for the preservation of liberty; it was an appeal to tradition. "I have but one lamp by which my feet are guided and that is the lamp of experience. I know of no way of judging of the future but by the past." Liberty was nothing more than a word to describe the political systems and the social order to which Henry and his compatriots were accustomed. They did, after all, live in the freest land in the world, and the moment the customary relationship between the freemen and the government changed, Henry was willing to call for action, first through petition, then by arms. His motivation was to arrest unconstitutional innovations in government, not to expound upon the general "rights of man." Henry was no egalitarian philosopher. He was a man of action in a time of action.

His political career after the War echoed his efforts in leading to independence. Henry believed Northern commercial interests to be a threat to the agrarian South, particularly when a cabal of Northern States attempted to secretly negotiate a treaty with Spain which would have surrendered American navigation rights to the Mississippi River. Union, in his mind, meant that each State—and by default each section—should benefit equally from the arrangement, and no one section, State, or people should be unjustly burdened by the other members of the confederation. Decentralization, then, served a purpose. Virginia could protect its people from money-grubbing Bay Staters, and the people of Pennsylvania, if they chose, could be free to enact mercantile schemes without interference from agrarian North Carolina. After all, the happiness, safety, and well-being of Virginians were protected by their own constitution and bill of rights, written and ratified before the Article of Confederation had been proposed and adopted.

Henry was asked to lead the Virginia delegation to the Philadelphia Convention in 1787. He declined, thinking he "smelled a rat." When the Constitution was brought back to the people of Virginia for ratification, Henry led the charge against it. His June 5, 1788 speech should be required reading for every American. Henry declared that, "if twelve states and a half had adopted it, I would, with manly firmness, and in spite of an erring world, reject it…" and chastised proponents of the document for their lack of foresight. "You are not," he said, "to inquire how your trade may be increased, nor how you are to become a great and powerful people, but how your liberties can be secured; for liberty ought to be the direct end of your government." He cautioned his fellow delegates not to rush to judgment. History had shown "revolutions like this have happened in almost every country in Europe; similar examples are to be found in ancient Greece and ancient Rome — instances of the people losing their liberty by their own carelessness and the ambition of a few." And though he recognized that the Constitution may prevent "licentiousness," Henry warned, "there is another thing it will as effectually do — it will oppress and ruin the people."

Henry railed against congressional power over the militia and by default the potential for the central authority to disarm the people, and against the executive, an office he considered to be little more than a thinly veiled monarchy. Most of this speech, however, was an appeal to the people of Virginia, both present and future, to resist a headlong charge to tyranny. "The voice of tradition, I trust, will inform posterity of our struggles for freedom. If our descendants be worthy the name of Americans, they will preserve, and hand down to their latest posterity, the transactions of the present times; and, though I confess my exclamations are not worthy the hearing, they will see that I have done my utmost to preserve their liberty; for I never will give up the power of direct taxation but for a scourge." Prophetically, Henry warned that according to the Constitution, "the preservation of our liberty depends on the single chance of men being virtuous enough to make laws to punish themselves." Time has proven his fears were justified.

Henry's closing remarks emphasized that the Constitution without amendments violated the principles of 1776, and he feared that even with amendments the people and the States would not be sufficiently protected against centralization and tyranny. He hoped "that the spirit which predominated in the revolution is not yet gone, nor the cause of those who are attached to the revolution yet lost." Sadly, that spirit has long been buried, and Henry's sagacious remarks have gone unheeded by subsequent generations. Yet, it is not too late to rekindle Henry's devotion to liberty and to the ancient traditions that defined his generation. Let us honor his birthday with a toast he would support, "To those who fight for the Principles of '76, present and future, and to the eternal principle of liberty."

The United States Is (Are) Not A Nation!

I HAVE OFTEN REQUIRED my students on the first day or two of class to use the *Oxford English Dictionary* and define the following words: nation and state. Most do not follow my directions and submit a modern *Webster*'s or online distortion of the word, and those who use the *Oxford* often fail to provide the etymology of either word. I can't fault them for that, because they have probably been taught since first grade in the public "school" system to submit the first definition they find. Thus, the common results of the activity are similar to the following:

Nation – noun: a large body of people, associated with a particular territory, that is sufficiently conscious of its unity to seek or to possess a government peculiarly its own. (from dictionary.com)

State – noun: the territory, or one of the territories, of a government. (from dictionary.com)

How profound, statist…and completely absurd! If both are true, than the United States should simply be the "United State." A state is simply a "territory…of a government"? A nation is simply a large body of people that occupy a territory? That would be news to the founding generation. Of course, a careful reading of the history of both words could correct this mess and place the Union of the States within its proper historical context.

The word "nation" found its way into the English language around the 14th century. Under the old definition, a nation was a group of people who shared a similar racial, cultural, or religious background that often-included elements such as a common language. A State was a sovereign political entity, not simply a "territory…of a government." By viewing the United States through that lens, it becomes clear that modern definitions of nation and state are the product of centralization and the mischaracterization of the federal government as a "national government."

Part I: The Jeffersonian Tradition

Certainly no one in the founding generation would have argued that Virginia and Massachusetts possessed the same cultural heritage. Virginia, with its strong Cavalier tradition, and Massachusetts, with its Puritan or roundhead foundations, were clearly at odds during the seventeenth century and beyond. The two colonies may have been populated by white, English Christians and who shared a common language, "English," but as David Hackett Fischer beautifully explained in his *Albion's Seed*, the two cultures were diametrically opposed in almost every conceivable way. From dress to food to speech, Virginia Cavaliers and Massachusetts Yankees were in many ways two separate nations, not simply separate cultures. The "shining city upon a hill" Puritans and their decedents never let Southerners forget their differences, nor did Southerners want to be lumped together with self-righteous Yankees. William Berkeley, the dominant figure in Virginia during the seventeenth century, despised Puritans and fought against them in the English Civil War. Later American sectionalism was little more than an explicit recognition of cultural differences and the existence of separate nations in North America dating to the early days of English settlement.

Adding to this American cultural cornucopia were the Celts, the Quakers, American Indian tribes, and African slaves, groups that had interesting and culturally significant contributions to the fabric of their respective regions as well. Thus, America in the colonial period was "multicultural" in a way that extended beyond race or religion. Western civilization and the English tradition dominated, but separate nations blotted the North American landscape. One of the most respected American historians on slavery, Eugene Genovese, wrote this about American culture in his *Roll, Jordan, Roll*: "Blacks and whites in America may be viewed as one nation or two, or as a nation within a nation, but their common history guarantees that, one way or another, they are both American." This statement accentuates the point that the phrase "American nation" is a rhetorical fabrication of the last 150 years of American history.

This was not lost on the founding generation. John Adams once wrote that, "I expressly say that Congress is not a representative body but a diplomatic body, a collection of ambassadors from thirteen sovereign States...." Each state had its own political and cultural life and each was "sovereign." Robert Yates, writing as Brutus in 1787, observed that "In a republic, the manners, sentiments, and interests of the people should be similar. If this not be the case, there will be a constant clashing of opinions; and the representatives of one part will be continually striving against those of the other." If applied to the United States, Yates concluded that:

> The United States includes a variety of climates. The productions of the different parts of the union are very variant, and their

interests of consequence, diverse. Their manners and habits differ as much as their climates and productions; and their sentiments are by no means coincident. The laws and customs of the several states are, in many respects, very diverse, and in some opposite; each would be in favor of its own interests and customs, and, of consequence, a legislature, formed of representatives from the respective parts, would not only be too numerous to act with any care of decision, but would be composed of such heterogeneous and discordant principles, as would constantly be contending with each other.

Of course, there were "nationalists" in the early federal period, but even they often understood that if the United States contained several nations rather than one, it would be better to separate than to consolidate. Gouverneur Morris, one of the most important "nationalists" (and womanizers) of this era, made the following statement during the Philadelphia Convention of 1787, "But, to come more to the point – either this distinction [between the Northern and Southern States] is fictitious or real; if fictitious, let it be dismissed, and let us proceed with due confidence. If it be real, instead of attempting to blend incompatible things, let us at once take a friendly leave of each other. There can be no end of demands for security, if every particular interest is to be entitled to it." And George Washington, often showcased as a fine example of the early "nationalists" and the glue that held the States together, said this about the people of Massachusetts in the early days of the War for Independence, "There is no nation under the sun that pays more adoration to money than they do."

States' rights and the Tenth Amendment to the Constitution were intended to protect this cultural distinctiveness, and secession was often seen as the only hedge against aggression from other States or sections. This is why the three most powerful States in 1788, Virginia in the South, New York in the mid-Atlantic, and Massachusetts in the North, considered an explicit recognition of States' rights an essential condition for ratification of the Constitution. Of course, those who champion States' rights and decentralization are often accused of preferring "Balkanization" over the blessings and security of "one nation." If the federal government followed its limited, constituted authority, such "Balkanization" would not be necessary, but hardly anyone in the founding generation would have agreed to a system of central government that currently exists in the United States. As Morris said in 1787, it would be better to separate than to subject one nation to the cultural imperialism of another State, section, or nation. Modern Americans have never been taught that lesson.

Why the Tenth Amendment?

THE RECENT REJUVENATION of interest in State's rights, nullification, and secession has been a welcome result of the explosion of federal power since the housing and credit bubbles burst last fall. The 10th Amendment movements and "tea parties" are, at least on one level, a pure form of "republicanism." Unfortunately, there are those who call themselves Republicans who have little understanding about the history of the republic, namely how the Founding generation conceptualized the "united States" as Jefferson called it in the Declaration of Independence. "Country club" Republican "protesters" have jumped on the bandwagon, and as folks on the LRC have documented, these individuals are purely pawns for the demagogues in the GOP, a party that has never truly been either for State's rights or limited government. Simply rallying against unconstitutional taxes, expansive federal programs, or shallow assaults on the Democrats and Barack Obama is not enough. You can chant about the 10th Amendment till you go hoarse, but without understanding the principles behind State sovereignty, your voice will be useless.

It becomes clear, then, that those who push for reasserting State power must know how the Founders defined a republic in both size and scope and what they meant by republicanism. Returning to the founding principles of the United States is an obvious way to end the insanity in Washington D.C., but it won't happen if State's rights are consistently viewed as a knee-jerk reactionary response to unconstitutional federal legislation. Yes, the 10th Amendment was included in the Bill of Rights, but *why* did the Founders insist on state sovereignty? Rather than a theoretical fabrication at the 1787 Philadelphia Convention or the State ratification conventions, State's rights were explicitly linked to the stability of the

United States from the Revolutionary War forward. That is the key to the State sovereignty movement.

Thomas Jefferson made two interesting statements concerning republics in 1816. In a letter to fellow Virginian John Taylor – one of the most insightful political economists and theorists of his day – Jefferson said that a republic "is evidently restrained to very narrow limits of space and population. I doubt if it would be practicable beyond the extent of a New England township." He also told Isaac Tiffany that "A democracy [is] the only pure republic, but impracticable beyond the limits of a town." In other words, a republic is only plausible over a small distance. Anything beyond that would destroy the ability of the people to control the government, and that is the foundation of republicanism. Jefferson wrote in the Declaration of Independence that legislative powers were "incapable of Annihilation" because "they return to the People at large for their exercise." State and local governments were most responsive to the people and thus the most republican in form.

To the Founders, diffusing power over large groups of people and then placing it in a small number of representatives violated the principle of direct control of the government, and more importantly, the Founders understood that the States stood as a hedge against factionalism. George Mason, speaking at the Philadelphia Convention, succinctly addressed this issue: "From the nature of man, we may be sure that those who have power in their hands will not give it up, while they can retain it. On the contrary, we know that they will always, when they can, rather increase it." Only the States could check arbitrary abuse of power which is one reason why Mason said he would rather cut off his right hand than sign the Constitution without a bill of rights. Factions, either sectional or personal, could destroy the interests of the people without recourse; the States provided that recourse.

Thus, the founding generation believed that the United States was nothing more than a federal union formed solely for defense and commerce. John Taylor, writing in his *Tyranny Unmasked*, explained that "the experiment of a consolidated republic, over a territory so extensive as the United States, is at least awful, when we can recollect no case in which it has been successful. If the people had believed it practicable, it would have been preferred to our system of division and union...." Patrick Henry argued during the Virginia ratification convention that State sovereignty was the only safeguard against the "infinitude" of the Constitution. He declared that "the delegation of power to an adequate number of representatives, and an unimpeded reversion of it back to the people, at short periods, form the principal traits of a republican government," and feared that the Constitution would lead to despotism and the subversion of republican principles.

The number of Americans who consistently believe their vote does not count on the federal level is a testament to the fact that the people have truly lost their hold on the "representatives" in Washington. Jefferson, Taylor, Mason, and Henry all understood that the people had greater control over their State and local representatives. They lived among them, went to church with them, socialized with them, and maybe even had family ties. Four hundred people protesting in Washington D.C. won't make a difference, but four hundred people protesting in front of the local courthouse will. It was, and is, simple economy of scale. Henry said, "The governing persons are the servants of the people." State sovereignty ensured that they remained the servants of the people and that the culture and customs of local communities would be preserved.

And, this wasn't just a component of Southern political philosophy. Northerners relied on State's rights to protect their local traditions, too. John Adams once wrote that he considered federal representatives to be nothing more than "ambassadors" from the several states. Gouverneur Morris of Pennsylvania, one of most ardent nationalists at the Philadelphia convention, considered the Senate as originally designed before the perversion of the 17th Amendment offered the only protection for the commercial States of the East. Moreover, if the sections could not mesh politically, he urged the following: "instead of attempting to blend incompatible things, let us at once take a friendly leave of each other." That was 1787. Roger Sherman of Connecticut considered the Articles of Confederation to be insufficient for the facilitation of commerce and defense, but he thought the powers of the States should be protected in order to safeguard the cultural integrity of each community. "Each state, like each individual, had its peculiar habits, usages, and manners, which constituted its happiness. It would not, therefore, give to others a power over this happiness, any more than an individual would do, when he could avoid it." Even Alexander Hamilton once said that the federal government could not coerce a State. Incidentally, Massachusetts conditionally ratified the Constitution with the understanding that a bill of rights would be added. State sovereignty was number one on the list.

Jefferson affirmed that the States were "FREE AND INDEPENDENT" in the Declaration of Independence. Nothing changed that, not the Constitution or efforts to reduce State influence and power by successive generations. Instead of focusing on the narrow issues of taxes and "big government," advocates of the 10th Amendment movement should emphasize that the State is the most responsive level of government, the most democratic, the purest form of a republic, and the political entity most able to ensure republican principles, which Jefferson listed as "simplicity, economy, religious and civil freedom." All the Founders would agree.

Decentralization for Socialists: A Brief Primer

ONE THING THAT CONSISTENTLY vexes me is the amount of time the modern statists, particularly on the Left, spend labeling the idea of decentralization and secession as "kooky." The Virginia and Kentucky Resolutions of 1798 – if they have read them or know about them – are often portrayed as quaint and unsophisticated pronouncements of provincialism; the Essex Junto and Hartford Convention are called the products of deranged Northern madmen; Andrew Jackson, they say, was on the right side when he threatened the use of force to keep South Carolinian secessionists in line in 1832; and of course, they revel in the ultimate *coup de grâce* to states' rights and secession, the Northern victory in the War for Southern Independence. Who could root for the evil, "undemocratic slave power" clad in butternut, anyway?

This would be well and good if their arguments were logical. They of course forget that the South seceded through a democratic process, but beyond that, one only has to look at the history of American socialists and reformers to find that many of them were secessionists and viewed decentralization as the logical path to their "utopian" society. The case of the failed "utopian" experiment Brook Farm in Roxbury, Massachusetts nicely illustrates how convoluted the Leftist argument against secession has become.

Brook Farm was established by George Ripley and his wife, Sophia, in 1841. They were transcendentalists who believed in the socialist ideology of Frenchman Charles Fourier, the intellectual progenitor of modern feminism. The Ripley's devised an autonomous community that emphasized a communal lifestyle in the pursuit of leisure. Every resident was to share equally in the task of growing products for market in order to maximize the time each individual could spend at leisure and learning. Sophia Ripley also ran the communal school. What they found is that most preferred leisure to work and a handful of the residents kept the rest afloat. Part of the commune ultimately burned down, and the Brook Farm "closed" in 1847.

But Brook Farm illustrated how socialist utopians viewed secession, or the removal from society, as the best means to practice their societal values. Fourier ultimately believed that no more than 1600 people should be involved in a single commune and each commune would be autonomous with only a loose confederation to oversee the entire process. In other words, there was very little large-scale centralization and tremendous decentralization, which they rightly viewed as the most democratic method of government.

Additionally, abolitionists consistently called for secession during the 1840s and 1850s. William Lloyd Garrison, for example, demanded an end to the Union in 1843. Henry David Thoreau simply seceded from society at Walden Pond. Other "reform" communities in New York's "burnt over" district sought the protection secession offered for their way of life. Secession need not come from an established political entity to exist in fact. These groups in many ways viewed themselves as autonomous and democratic societies operating in disobedience of laws they considered unjust. John Noyes and many of his followers were eventually run out of Oneida, New York for partaking in group marriage, a practice that violated the moral sensibilities of the rest of the state, but something the community believed was perfectly justifiable and natural. By flaunting their independent religious community and thumbing their nose at the state government, the Oneida community ultimately practiced a form of *de facto* secession from New York.

The same could be said for many individuals who headed west in the nineteenth century. Several towns operated outside the limits of the law, and federal or state power was often non-existent. "Boom towns" often exemplified the anything-goes spirit of the West, though in time churches, banks, schools, and other civilizing entities would show up. Even then, things remained fairly "rough" as long as the gold and silver kept pouring out of the mines. These were virtually independent communities and many of the people who resided there were interested in evading government for one reason or another. The West offered anonymity and protection from government abuse. The Mormons, who headed to Utah after being kicked out of Illinois, chose the West for that very reason and ultimately went to war with the United States – and threatened secession – after they were placed under the federal heel. But in spirit, they were already independent and had their own laws and government in place.

These were not "right wing" groups by modern standards, particularly the "reform" communes in New York and Massachusetts, but they understood that decentralization offered a hedge against alien threats to their society and lifestyle. Thomas Naylor of Vermont, hardly a "right winger," has been trumpeting the idea of an independent Vermont for almost a decade. He has recognized that the lifestyle Vermont citizens want to enjoy will be consistently retarded by imperial bureaucrats in Washington D.C. This only makes sense. If Californians, for example, want universal health care, have at it, but don't expect the people of Alabama to pay for it. If New York wants to severely curtail private gun ownership, go for it, but don't subject the people of Georgia to the same loss of civil liberty. That is how federalism should work and is how the founding generation designed it to work.

Leftists would do well to remember that their complaints about a slow and unresponsive federal government could be solved by decentralization. They have more control over state and local governments and could implement their utopian vision of an egalitarian society more quickly and easily. And, if you don't like where you live, you can always move to a more suitable republic of your choice. There would be plenty of "conservative" and "liberal" republics to choose from in North America.

Of course, as we all know, modern state socialism is an ideology of power, money, and statism, which is why its "champions" at the federal level, the "progressives," will never allow decentralization to infiltrate their political vocabulary; however, if enough Americans could be rightly persuaded that Washington is not the answer, either for "conservative" or "liberal" causes, then maybe the people would be willing to part ways and allow the Left to dominate the Northeast and West Coast and the Right to control the South and Mountain States. This is a peaceful, just, and democratic solution to a centuries-old problem. Let the people of each sovereign state decide their own fate. As Thomas Jefferson said in 1801, "If there be any among us who would wish to dissolve this Union or to change its republican form, let them stand undisturbed as monuments to the safety with which error of opinion may be tolerated where reason is left free to combat it."

Let's Give Up on the (Unwritten) Constitution

GEORGETOWN LAW PROFESSOR Louis Michael Seidman created a bit of a stir recently with a December 30 op-ed in the *New York Times* titled "Let's Give Up on the Constitution." He was the subject of a similar piece for *The Chronicle Review* in mid-December titled "The Constitution: Who Needs It?" Both articles support his forthcoming book, *On Constitutional Disobedience*, a sweeping challenge to the United States Constitution. In essence, Seidman contends that because the Constitution has been disregarded for several decades, Americans should cease to pay homage to an outmoded document littered with structural problems and open to diametrically opposed interpretations, i.e. originalism and "living constitutionalism." The American people, he said, are "at a stage where there is a growing realization that a lot of constitutional law is empty posturing." He added, "This is not a stable situation." Translation: the written Constitution is dead and because our "unwritten" constitution has served Americans quite well, we should ignore the written document and follow common law precedence. If the general government in Washington passes an unconstitutional law, Seidman contends "each of us should answer with a perfectly straight-forward, but deeply subversive, two word question: 'So What?'"

Seidman makes several valid points in both pieces and in this interview, but his solution – the recognition and acceptance of the "unwritten" constitution – is dangerous, and more importantly his belief in a "national" American polity is the inherent weakness of the "unwritten" model.

Sideman told Megyn Kelly of Fox News that he opposes gun control legislation not because it is unconstitutional, but because it does not work, and he thinks that Americans should support free speech in the abstract, not because a piece of parchment "gives" that right to Americans. I agree on both points. If Americans considered gun ownership to be a natural right of self-preservation and self-defense, as William Blackstone famously called it in his commentaries on English law, then the current debate on gun control would not be taking place. Additionally, if the American public (and by default the central government) believed in reciprocal civil liberty, then there would be no need for the Bill of Rights. But they don't and historically never have. That was the greatest rallying cry for a Bill of Rights in 1787 and 1788. As Thomas Tredwell of New York said in his State Ratifying Convention in 1788 in arguing against the Constitution devoid of a Bill of Rights:

> In this Constitution, sir, we have departed widely from the principles and political faith of '76 when the spirit of liberty ran high, and danger put a curb on ambition. Here we find no security for the rights of individuals, no security for the existence of our state governments; here is no bill of rights, no proper restriction of power; our lives, our property, and our consciences, are left wholly at the mercy of the legislature, and the powers of the judiciary may be extended to any degree short of almighty. Sir, in this Constitution we have not only neglected – we have done worse – we have openly violated, our faith – that is, our public faith.

Without a codification of those rights, Tredwell and others believed that the general government would run roughshod over American civil liberties and the sovereignty of the States.

Of course, Seidman can point to arguments *against* a Bill of Rights in support of his position. Both Alexander Hamilton and James Wilson thought that an enumeration of such rights would allow the government to abuse others. As Hamilton wrote, "Why for instance, should it be said, that the liberty of the press shall not be restrained, when no power is given by which such restrictions may be imposed? I will not contend that such a provision would confer a regulating power; but it is evident that it would furnish, to men disposed to usurp, a plausible pretence for claiming that power." Hamilton was working on the assumption – and a disingenuous one – that the government would abide by the written limits of the document. Yet, those written limits would disappear if the Constitution was scrapped in favor of the unwritten British model. Civil liberty would have to rely on the public at large for enforcement and judging by the current state of political discourse in the United States, that would be a frightening scenario. It would take a dramatic educational paradigm shift to make most Americans believe that their fellow citizens at large are interested in the preservation of their rights. The founding generation understood that as well, which is why in addition to both governing documents for the United States, the Articles of Confederation and the United States Constitution, every State wrote a Constitution in the founding period.

Siedman is also correct that the Framers made amending the Constitution exceedingly difficult. This was pointed out both in Philadelphia in 1787 and in several of the State ratifying conventions. The Constitution was amended twelve times by the founding generation including the Bill of Rights, but only fifteen times since. Yet, if the Constitution was followed as ratified, then amending the Constitution would become irrelevant. The States, equipped with their own codified bill of rights and armed with the sovereignty and legitimacy of the people, handled all domestic issues, moral, legal, and political. Decentralization, in other words, prevented the need for amendments.

Anyone who lives in Alabama can attest to the problems presented by a strongly centralized government and a constitution that is outrageously simple to amend. At last count, the Alabama State Constitution had over 850 amendments. Local governments cannot sneeze without permission from the State. That is what Americans would be (and are) subjected to under the current unwritten Untied States Constitution. All issues would become, by default, national issues, which is what Siedman wants. Nationalism, "this (meaning the singular United States) is *our* country," creates an inherently uncivil climate in relation to the individual and the rights, customs, and cultures of the local community. An unwritten national Constitution may work among a generally homogenous population, but never over a diverse region like the United States. Joseph Taylor of North Carolina spoke for many in the founding generation, North and South, when he said in 1788, "We see plainly that men who come from New England are different from us. They are ignorant of our situation; they do not know the state of our country [North Carolina]. They cannot with safety legislate for us." Bay Staters thought the same of their Tar Heel counterparts. Nothing has changed. The "Chicago way" is not the Alabama way – thank God.

The unwritten Constitution that Siedman glorifies has led to the trampling of civil liberties, the suppression of free government, the destruction of individual rights, and the centralization of power in the hands of 545 elected and unelected oligarchs. What the American political system needs is a good dose of federalism and decentralization and a return to the Constitution *as ratified* through the Tenth Amendment. As Kirkpatrick Sale recently said in this video, "The problems that we face now, there's not a one of them that could not be solved or at least ameliorated considerably if we didn't face it at a smaller scale." I agree with Siedman that the Constitution of the founding generation is dead and that no one follows it, but by capitulating to the "So What?" mindset, the American experiment of limited, written, decentralized constitutional government would meet its ultimate doom. We might as well raise a toast to "God Save the Queen!" and forget that Washington, Henry, Adams, Jefferson, Rutledge, Dickinson, Franklin, or Sherman even existed.

Our Conservative Constitution

IN THE LAST WEEK, the left has orchestrated a public assault on the Constitution. This is nothing new, but the offensive is noteworthy because it involved both a Supreme Court justice and the president of the United States. On January 30, Supreme Court Justice Ruth Bader Ginsburg said during a television interview in Egypt that, "I would not look to the United States Constitution if I were drafting a constitution in the year 2012." Six days later, President Barack Obama told Matt Lauer that, "I have not been able to force Congress to implement every aspect of what I said in 2008 ... it turns out that our founders designed a system that makes it more difficult to bring about change than I would like sometimes." And the following day, *New York Times* contributor Adam Liptak wrote that, "The Constitution has seen better days. ... The United States Constitution is terse and old, and it guarantees relatively few rights."

To progressives, the Constitution serves as a continual impediment to their legislative agenda. Liptak continued in his piece that perhaps there are "newer, sexier, and more powerful operating systems in the constitutional marketplace." In other words, the Constitution is an archaic relic that needs to be discarded and replaced with something better. Obama essentially said the same thing in his State of the Union address when he called the executive branch "outdated." This tune has been played before, both by the left and more importantly by James Madison in 1787.

The standard interpretation of the 1787 Constitutional Convention in Philadelphia has "large state" advocates such as James Madison of Virginia pitted against "small state" proponents like William Paterson of New Jersey. According to this narrative, the small states, such as Delaware, New Jersey, Maryland, and

South Carolina, were concerned that larges states such as Virginia, New York, and Massachusetts, were attempting a power grab in Philadelphia through Madison's famous Virginia Plan. It would have scrapped the Articles of Confederation — the first governing document for the United States — and replaced it with a Constitution that had a bicameral legislature with representation based on population in both houses, a supreme court, and an executive branch. Madison was searching for a "newer, sexier, more powerful operating system." He would not get his wish. His constitution fell apart almost immediately after it was presented by Edmund Randolph in the opening days of the convention.

The conservative backlash against Madison's plan was led by men like John Dickinson of Delaware, Roger Sherman of Connecticut, Luther Martin of Maryland, George Mason of Virginia, and John Rutledge of South Carolina. Madison is often called the "father of the Constitution," but the final document had more of Sherman, Dickinson, and Rutledge in it than Madison. Dickinson famously said during the Convention that "Experience must be our only guide. Reason may mislead us." This was a slap at Madison's "reasonable" changes to the central government. Dickinson later added that, "If the state governments were excluded from all agency in the national one, and all power drawn from the people at large, the consequence would be, that the national government would move in the same direction as the state governments now do, and would run into the same mischiefs" such as depreciated paper currency, high taxes, and oppressive legislation. Sound familiar?

The real debate in Philadelphia, then, was not between large states and small states; it was between nationalists and federalists. The nationalists, such as Madison, Alexander Hamilton, James Wilson, and Gouverneur Morris, wanted to abolish the states and create a singular central government charged with legislating for the American people as a whole. The federalists (often misslabeled the anti-federalists) resisted, and while they were willing to give the central government greater strength, they insisted that the states retain control of the government with the exception of certain delegated or enumerated powers. They won the debate, as proponents of the Constitution continually pointed out during the ratification process. As William Richardson Davie of North Carolina said in 1788 in arguing *for* the ratification of the Constitution, "If there were any seeds in this Constitution which might, one day, produce a consolidation, it would, sir, with me, be an insuperable objection. I am so perfectly convinced that so extensive a country as this can never be managed by one consolidated government."

Americans need to redefine how they think of the central government. The founding generation called it a "general" government charged with general purposes for the States United. The states, as the Tenth Amendment to the Constitution clearly illustrates, retained all power not delegated to the central authority. So, what did the founders call "general" purposes? Roger Sherman, the man who added the infamous "general welfare clause" to the Constitution (which was simply lifted from the Articles of Confederation), argued it was nothing more than defense, both internal and external, trade, and commerce with "All other matters, civil and criminal" left "in the hands of the states." David Ramsey of South Carolina suggested that the "powers of Congress ... may be referred to this single principle, 'that the general concerns of the *union* [not individuals] ought to be managed by the general government." (Emphasis added.) Madison said in 1791 that giving Congress unlimited power "would render nugatory the enumeration of particular powers [and] would supercede all the powers reserved to the state governments."

Of course, if the states delegated authority to the general government, they had to first possess it and by delegating power they still retained it. A delegated power can be rescinded. The states, or the people of the states in convention, consented to the Constitution because it was and is a constitution "for the United States" and "between the States so ratifying the same." The Constitution established a union of states. The founding generation, with a few exceptions, feared a "national" government that could micromanage every municipality and county in the union. Even an ardent nationalist like James Wilson recognized this when he said in the 1787 Pennsylvania ratifying convention that "To support with vigor, a single government over the whole extent of the United States, would demand a system of the most unqualified and the most unremitted despotism." A limited government that handled only the general concerns of the union allowed the states to govern their domestic concerns freely and without interference from the central authority.

The beauty of the founding fathers' Constitution *as ratified* by the states in 1787 and 1788 is that it allowed for the greatest liberty and independence of the people. Many considered a bill of rights unnecessary, for example, because the states already had their own and thus the general government could never infringe on the liberty of the people, and because the *states* protected that liberty by serving as a hedge between the people and a tyrannical central authority. In short, another bill of rights was redundant. When Madison finally put the Bill of Rights to a vote in Congress, he wanted to incorporate them into the state constitutions but was resoundingly defeated, not because the other members of the Congress desired a tyranny at home, but because their liberties were *already legally protected at home.*

The union of the founders was a conservative union that respected differences among the states and the people of the states. Three states had established churches in 1787 while others, like Virginia, enjoyed religious freedom. Every state viewed the penal code differently. Every state had differences in citizenship and voting requirements. The cultures of each state were protected by a general union for general purposes. As the ardent proponent of the Constitution Tench Coxe wrote in 1788:

> The several states can create corporations civil and religious ... establish seminaries of learning; erect boroughs, cities, and counties; promote and establish manufacturers; open roads; clear rivers; cut canals; regulate descents and marriages; licence taverns ... establish ferries; erect public buildings ... establish poor houses, hospitals, and house of employment; regulate the police; and many other things of utmost importance to the happiness of their respective citizens. In short, besides the particulars enumerated, every thing of a domestic nature must or can be done by them.

And by default, Coxe also added that the general government could not do any of these things or "do any other matter or thing appertaining to the internal affairs of any state, whether legislative, executive, or judicial, civil or ecclesiastical." How refreshing. If Americans, left and right, relied on the federal principles of the Constitution *as ratified* by the states, then they would have nothing to fear from the general government. Socialists could have their utopia in California or Massachusetts while conservatives would be shielded from that type of society in Alabama or Mississippi. That would be the most democratic course to follow.

The rub today is not between socialists and capitalists as some would suggest. It is the age-old debate between nationalists and federalists that began in 1787 at the Philadelphia Convention. Obama, Ginsburg, and the progressives (those on the right included) are nationalists bent on centralizing power in Washington, D.C. and destroying the states. They use terms such as civil rights, diversity, and equality to mask their agenda of establishing a "United State" with a unified culture under their guiding hand. They implicitly recognize by denouncing the Constitution that the founding generation opposed consolidation, and rightly so. The left argues that it is "reasonable" to conclude that the "national" government needs reform and perhaps a new Constitution. Madison said the same thing, but his experiment in government had been attempted before, and history had shown that extreme centralization, which is what the nationalists wanted, always resulted in tyranny. Americans should be thankful that men like John Dickinson won the day and should resist the "reasonable" urge to adopt a "sexier" system that would only give us more centralization and more government. As the famous opponent of the Constitution "An Old Whig" wrote in 1787:

> It is a matter of immense consequence, in establishing a government which is to last for ages, and which, if it be suffered to depart from the principles of liberty in the beginning, will in all probability, never return to them, that we consider carefully what sort of government we are about to form. Power is very easily increased; indeed it naturally grows in every government but it hardly ever lessens.

Who's Supreme:
The Supremacy Clause Smackdown

WHEN IDAHO GOVERNOR C.L. "Butch" Otter signed HO391 into law on 17 March 2010, the "national" news media circled the wagons and began another assault on State sovereignty. The bill required the Idaho attorney general to sue the federal government over insurance mandates in the event national healthcare legislation passed. The lead AP reporter on the story, John Miller, quoted constitutional "scholar" David Freeman Engstrom of Stanford Law School as stating that the Idaho law would be irrelevant because of the "supremacy clause" of the United States Constitution.

In his words, "That language is clear that federal law is supreme over state law, so it really doesn't matter what a state legislature says on this." Now that Barack Obama has signed healthcare legislation into law, almost a dozen States have filed suit against the federal government, with Idaho in the lead. Battle lines have been drawn. Unfortunately, the question of State sovereignty and the true meaning of the "supremacy clause" may be swallowed up in the ensuing debate.

Engstrom's opinion is held by a majority of constitutional law "scholars," but he is far from correct, and Idaho and the thirty seven other States considering similar legislation have a strong case based on the original intent of the powers of the federal government vis-a-vis the States.

The so-called "supremacy clause" of the Constitution, found in Article 6, states, "This Constitution, and the Laws of the United States *which shall be made in Pursuance thereof*; and all Treaties made, or which shall be made, under the Authority of the United States, shall be the supreme Law of the Land; and the Judges in every State shall be bound thereby, any Thing in the Constitution or Laws of any State to the Contrary notwithstanding [emphasis added]."

The key, of course, is the italicized phrase. All laws made in pursuance of the Constitution, or those clearly enumerated in the document, were supreme, State laws notwithstanding. In other words, the federal government was supreme in all items clearly listed in the document.

A quick reading of the Constitution illustrates that national healthcare is not one of the enumerated powers of the federal government, so obviously Engstrom's blanket and simplistic statement is blatantly incorrect, but his distortion of the supremacy clause goes further.

The inclusion of such a clause in the Constitution was first debated at the Constitutional Convention on 31 May 1787. In Edmund Randolph's initial proposal, called the Virginia Plan, the "national" legislature had the ability to "legislate in all cases to which the separate states are incompetent" and "to negative all laws passed by the several states contravening, in the opinion of the national legislature, the Articles of Union." John Rutledge, Pierce Butler, and Charles Pinckney of South Carolina challenged the word "incompetent" and demanded that Randolph define the term. Butler thought that the delegates "were running into an extreme, in taking away the powers of the states" through such language.

Randolph replied that he "disclaimed any intention *to give indefinite powers to the national legislature,* declaring that he was entirely opposed to such an inroad on the state jurisdictions, and that he did not think any considerations whatever could ever change his determination [emphasis added]." James Madison, the author of the Virginia Plan, was not as forthcoming as to his sentiment. Ultimately, Madison preferred a negative over State law and wished the national legislature to be supreme in call cases. But he was not in the majority.

The Convention again broached a federal negative on State law on 8 June 1787. Charles Pinckney, who presented a draft of a constitution shortly after Randolph offered the Virginia Plan, believed a national negative necessary to the security of the Union, and Madison, using imagery from the solar system and equating the sun to the national government, argued that without a national negative, the States "will continually fly out of their proper orbits, and destroy the order and harmony of the political system." Such symbolism made for a beautiful picture, but it belied reality.

To most of the assembled delegates, the national government was not the center of the political universe and the States retained their sovereignty. Hugh Williamson of North Carolina emphatically stated he "was against giving a power that might restrain the states from regulating their internal police."

Elbridge Gerry of Massachusetts was against an unlimited negative, and Gunning Bedford of Delaware believed a national negative was simply intended "to strip the small states of their equal right of suffrage." He asked, "Will not these large states crush the small ones, whenever they stand in the way of their ambitious or interested views?"

When the negative power was put to a vote, seven States voted against it and three for it, with Delaware divided (and Virginia only in the affirmative by one vote). Roger Sherman of Connecticut summarized the sentiment of the majority when he stated he "thought the cases in which the negative ought to be exercised might be defined." Since the negative did not pass, such a definition was unnecessary.

Thus, the federal government was supreme only in its enumerated powers and it did not have a negative over State law. Supremacy had limits.

By the time the Constitution was debated in the several State ratifying conventions in 1787 and 1788, the "supremacy clause" galvanized opponents of the document. The Constitution, they said, would destroy the States and render them impotent in their internal affairs. The response from *proponents* of ratification illuminates the true intent of the clause. William Davie, a delegate to the Constitutional Convention from North Carolina and proponent of the Constitution, responded to attacks levied on the "supremacy clause" by stating that:

This Constitution, *as to the powers therein granted*, is constantly to be the supreme law of the land. Every power ceded by it must be executed without being counteracted by the laws or constitutions of the individual states. *Gentlemen should distinguish that it is not the supreme law in the exercise of power not granted. It can be supreme only in cases consistent with the powers specially granted, and not in usurpations* [emphasis added].

Davie wasn't alone in this opinion. Future Supreme Court justice James Iredell of North Carolina argued that, "This clause [the supremacy clause] is supposed to give too much power, when, in fact, it only provides for the execution of those powers which *are already given in the foregoing articles*. If Congress, under pretence of executing one power, should, in fact, usurp another, they will violate the Constitution [emphasis added]."

Furthermore, in a foreshadowing of nullification, Iredell argued that, "It appears to me merely a general clause, the amount of which is that, when they [Congress] pass an act, if it be in the execution of a power given by the Constitution, it shall be binding on the people, *otherwise not* [emphasis added]. Other ratifying conventions had similar debates, and proponents of the Constitution continually reassured wavering supporters that the Constitution would only be supreme within its delegated authority.

Most bought their assurances, though to staunch opponents, the Constitution still vested too much power in the central authority. The States would lose their sovereignty, they argued, and as a result, these men demanded an amendment to the Constitution that expressly maintained the sovereignty of the States and placed limits on federal power. Even several moderate supporters of the Constitution embraced this idea.

Ultimately, the three most powerful States in the Union, New York, Massachusetts, and Virginia, demanded that a bill of rights be immediately added to the Constitution; near the top of those recommended amendments on every list, a State sovereignty resolution. These ultimately became the Tenth Amendment to the Constitution, which reads, "The powers not delegated to the United States by the Constitution, nor prohibited by it to the States, are reserved to the States respectively, or to the people."

Clearly the intent of this amendment was to mitigate any design the federal government had on enlarging its powers through the "supremacy clause." If the power was not enumerated in the Constitution and the States were not prohibited by the Constitution from exercising said power, then that power was reserved to the States.

Several other constitutional "scholars" have weighed in on the debate in the last week, and each has invoked the "supremacy clause" to defend their opposition to State action against healthcare. Duke Law Professor Neil Siegel went so far as to suggest that the States are not reading the Tenth Amendment correctly. In perhaps the most outlandish statement of the debate, he also said, "Any talk of nullification bothers me because it's talk of lawlessness."

I guess Mr. Siegel has failed to consider that Idaho bill HO391 was passed by a legitimate legislative body elected by the people of the State. That would make it lawful.

Of course, this debate ultimately boils down to loose interpretation verses strict construction. Thomas Jefferson had the best line on this issue. When asked to read between the lines to "find" implied powers, Jefferson responded that he had done that, and he found only blank space.

The original intent of both the "supremacy clause" and the Tenth Amendment indicate that Idaho and the other States challenging Obamacare are justified and correct and that the legal profession is either in the tank for the federal government or has not read either the debates of the Constitutional Convention and/or the State ratifying debates. This should make people like Engstrom and Siegel, rather than legitimate State law directed at unconstitutional authority, irrelevant.

Rewriting History:
A Response to Ian Millhiser's Diatribe on "Tentherism."

HOW MANY WAYS CAN PROGRESSIVES DISTORT and rewrite history? If you read a recent piece entitled "Doomed to Repeat History" by policy analyst Ian Millhiser at the progressive think tank Center for American Progress the answer would be countless. His inaccuracies, partisan propaganda, scare tactics, and mistruths scream for a response. Of course, the statist zombies who sop up progressive talking points will probably view Millhiser's work as the trump card against "tentherism," but that is the principal problem. Millhiser has no idea what he is talking about (surprise!). He does not understand the objectives of the Tenth Amendment movement and his definition of "tentherism" is hardly accurate. Perhaps he doesn't care, since demonizing those who support liberty and limited central government is what progressives do best, but Millhiser obviously needs an elementary lesson on the Tenth Amendment and American history in general.

Millhiser begins his piece by stating that "conservatives are over-reading the Tenth Amendment." This must not be allowed to happen, he contends, because "Tentherism is dangerous," "Tentherism has no basis in constitutional text or history," and "Tentherism is authoritarian." The first charge smacks of a statement Duke Law School professor Neil Siegel made in March when he called nullification "lawlessness." From the evidence, it appears Duke Law School graduates and professors (Millhiser received his J.D. from Duke) are well versed in statist propaganda but don't have a clue about the ratification of the Constitution or the original intent of the Tenth Amendment. The first and third can be refuted in tandem, but the second is where Millhiser ignores much of early American history and cherry picks individuals and events to fit his "tentherism" paradigm.

Fallacy #1:
"Tentherism Has No Basis In Constitutional History Or Text."

When the Constitution was sent to the thirteen "SOVEREIGN AND INDEPENDENT STATES"—as Thomas Jefferson called them in the Declaration of Independence—for ratification, it faced an uphill battle in the three most powerful States at the time, New York, Massachusetts, and Virginia. Early odds had it failing in all three. A handful of opponents in each State ended up switching their votes in favor of ratification because they were guaranteed a bill of rights would be added to the Constitution. Each of these States submitted a list of recommended amendments, and at the top of each list stood a State sovereignty amendment. Massachusetts' proposed first amendment read: "That it be explicitly declared, that all powers not expressly delegated by the aforesaid Constitution are reserved to the several states, to be by them exercised." Virginia's proposed first amendment stated: "That each state in the Union shall respectfully retain every power, jurisdiction, and right, which is not by this Constitution delegated to the Congress of the United States, or to the departments of the federal government." And New York's proposed fifth amendment demanded that "no power shall be exercised by Congress, but such as is expressly given by this Constitution; and all others, not expressly given, shall be reserved to the respective states, to be by them exercised." Maryland and South Carolina also submitted proposed State sovereignty amendments.

There you have it. Jefferson, a Founding Father, called the States "sovereign and independent" in America's first State's rights document, and five States submitted a State sovereignty amendment as a condition of ratification. The delegates were persuaded to refrain from stating amendments were a "pre-condition," but that was the point. These ultimately became the Tenth Amendment to the Constitution. And don't forget that North Carolina and Rhode Island did not ratify the Constitution until 1789 and 1790 respectively, thus making them independent countries for a time. That is the best expression of "tentherism." But the Tenth Amendment tradition goes further, and it includes other members of the founding generation, many of whom were ardent Federalists.

Founding Fathers Jefferson and James Madison laid the groundwork for the Tenth Amendment movement in 1798 by authoring the Virginia and Kentucky Resolves. Madison argued in the Virginia Resolves that "the powers of the general government" result "from the compact to which the states are parties, as limited by the plain sense and intention of the instrument constituting that compact," and are "no further valid than they are authorized by the grants enumerated in that compact...." As such, the States have the authority, under the Tenth Amendment, to "interpose, for arresting the progress of the evil, and for maintaining, within their respective limits, the authorities, rights, and liberties, appertaining to them." Interposition is another word for nullification, and it is based on the Tenth Amendment.

Jefferson was more direct in the Kentucky Resolves. He simply stated that the States "delegated to [the federal] government certain definite powers, reserving, each state to itself, the residuary mass of right to their own self-government; and that whensoever the general government assumes undelegated powers, its acts are unauthoritative, void, and of no force...." How did he come to this conclusion? It was "expressly declared by one of the amendments to the Constitution..." i.e., the Tenth Amendment. Jefferson and Madison probably knew something about American constitutional government. Of course, Millhiser illustrates Madison's inconsistency, a trait that marked his career, but Jefferson never backed down from this position.

And it wasn't just Jefferson and Madison who advanced the Tenth Amendment in the founding generation. Northerners used it to support their agenda against the federal government as well. Several members of the famous secessionist group called the Essex Junto and the later Hartford Convention that met during the waning months of the War of 1812 were from the founding generation. For example, George Cabot served as a delegate to the Massachusetts ratifying convention of 1788; Nathan Dane was a member of the Continental Congress; James Hillhouse served in the American War for Independence and in the United States Senate; Daniel Lyman served at the Battle of White Plains with George Washington; Samuel Ward served in the War for Independence and attended the Annapolis Convention of 1786 that sent in motion the Constitutional Convention; Timothy Pickering was United States Secretary of State and a patriot leader during the War; Fisher Ames was a member of the Massachusetts ratifying convention and served in the United States Congress; Francis Dana signed the Articles of Confederation, served in the Continental Congress and United States Congress and supported the Constitution at the Massachusetts ratifying convention; and Theophilus Parson wrote the set of proposed amendments at the Massachusetts ratifying convention in 1788 that persuaded a few opponents to support the Constitution. As with Jefferson and Madison, these men knew something about the Constitution and the Tenth Amendment, and all were Federalists.

In fact, in 1815, the Hartford Convention said the following in their report and resolutions:

> That acts of Congress in violation of the Constitution are absolutely void, is an undeniable position. It does not, however, consist with the respect and forbearance due from a confederate State towards the General Government, to fly to open resistance

upon every infraction of the Constitution. The mode and the energy of the opposition should always conform to the nature of the violation, the intention of its authors, the extent of the injury inflicted, the determination manifested to persist in it, and the danger of delay. But in cases of deliberate, dangerous, and palpable infractions of the Constitution, affecting the sovereignty of a State, and liberties of the people; it is not only the right but the duty of such a State to interpose its authority for their protection, in the manner best calculated to secure that end [emphasis added].

These Federalists nullified federal laws in support of the War. So, either Millhiser is ignorant of this history when he writes "Tentherism has no basis in constitutional text or history," or he purposely ignores it. It's probably the former. Either way, contrary to Millhiser's claims, the Tenth Amendment was firmly entrenched in the history of the founding period and it is entirely based on the text of the Constitution. Maybe Millhiser forgets that the Tenth Amendments is part of the Constitution, and to the States who proposed it, the Amendment limited the power of the federal government to delegated items or those listed in Article 1, Section 8 of the Constitution.

Fallacy #2:
The Founding Fathers Rejected "Tetherism."

Millhiser charges that regardless of how narrowly modern "tenthers" view the Constitution, members of the founding generation, including Washington, Alexander Hamilton, and John Marshall, along with the First Congress, thought otherwise. His uses two bills from the founding period as evidence: a 1790 law regulating commerce with the American Indian tribes and the incorporation of the First Bank of the United States in 1791. He takes the first out of context and murders the history of the second.

Millhiser contends that "Washington's decision to sign the [1790 Act to Regulate Trade and Intercourse with the Indian Tribes] demonstrates his expansive view of the commerce power—a view that in no way resembles tentherism." He argues that the act "reached far beyond economic matters…including wholly noneconomic crimes such as assault or murder." The bill was written in the midst of the Northwest Indian War, and Washington had insisted that Congress attempt to extend the olive branch to the Indian tribes in the hope that war could be eliminated. At the same time, Washington was planning a major military campaign against the tribes if hostilities continued. They did until 1795.

Rewriting History: A Response to Ian Millhiser's Diatribe on "Tentherism."

Most of the 1790 act was designed to regulate trade but the portion of the bill that Millhiser outlines was designed to regulate the "Intercourse" with the tribes and had nothing to do with commerce or the "commerce clause" of the Constitution. As the title suggests, it was a piece of legislation that accomplished two tasks, regulating "Trade *and* Intercourse." In the eighteenth century the word intercourse meant social dealings, so Washington's signature did not imply that he agreed with an "expansive view of the commerce power." It simply meant he didn't want Americans stirring hostilities through their "intercourse" with Indians while in Indian territory. Here is the text of that portion of the bill:

> That if any citizen or inhabitant of the United States, or of either of the territorial districts of the United States, shall go into any town, settlement or territory belonging to any nation or tribe of Indians, and shall there commit any crime upon, or trespass against, the person or property of any peaceable and friendly Indian or Indians, which, if committed within the jurisdiction of any state, or within the jurisdiction of either of the said districts, against a citizen or white inhabitant thereof, would be punishable by the laws of such state or district, such offender or offenders shall be subject to the same punishment, and shall be proceeded against in the same manner as if the offence had been committed within the jurisdiction of the state or district to which he or they may belong, against a citizen or white in habitant thereof.

Taking the language of the bill and the historical situation out of context, which Millhiser has done, to satisfy or support an agenda against the attack on national health care is irresponsible to say the least. Dishonest would be a better word, but again, maybe Millhiser is ignorant of the history. That wouldn't be shocking.

Millhiser's characterization of the debate over the incorporation of the First Bank of the United States in 1791 also suffers from historical inaccuracies. He contends that Madison opposed the plan because he worried about the "spending powers" of the federal government. Madison never opposed the Bank on those terms. In his words, if the Congress had the power to incorporate a bank, then "They could incorporate companies of manufacturers, or companies for cutting canals, or even religious societies...." This was a power the federal government did not possess. He anticipated that chartering a bank would have to be accomplished through the "general welfare clause" or the "necessary and proper clause" of the Constitution, and he considered both approaches fraudulent.

Madison advanced during both the debate over the Bank and later in his Virginia Resolves that the "general welfare" clause of the Constitution had been "copied from the very limited grant of powers in the former Articles of Confederation." This was true. In fact, during the Constitutional Convention in 1787, Gouverneur Morris of Pennsylvania attempted to enlarge the power of the central government under the "general welfare" but was blocked by Roger Sherman of Connecticut. The "general welfare clause" of the Constitution carried the same weight as the "general welfare clause" of the Articles of Confederation. In essence, only items listed in Article 1, Section 8 of the Constitution were for the "general welfare" of the Union, and a Bank of the United States was not one of them.

And Madison said in 1791 that the "necessary and proper clause" was "in fact merely declaratory of what would have resulted by unavoidable implication, as the appropriate, and, as it were, technical means of executing those powers. In this sense it has been explained by the friends of the Constitution and ratified by the State Conventions." Of course, Millhiser claims that there are "few, if any, substantive limits on Congress's [SIC] spending power" through the "general welfare clause," but that wasn't the main thrust of Madison's argument; moreover, Millhiser's characterization of the "general welfare clause" is incorrect according to most members of the founding generation, including the men who placed it in the Constitution.

When Washington received the bill for his signature, he was concerned that Madison considered the bill unconstitutional. He asked Jefferson and his Attorney General Edmund Randolph to submit their opinion on the issue. Jefferson's rebuke of the Bank centered on the not yet ratified Tenth Amendment to the Constitution. Washington believed Jefferson and concurrently asked Madison to write a veto message and Hamilton to submit an argument in favor of the Bank. He told Hamilton that he would only sign the bill if his arguments dwarfed Jefferson's. Washington ultimately sided with Hamilton, in part because he bought Hamilton's "loose construction" arguments, but also because Washington thought the issue more closely affected Hamilton's department. It must be said that Washington was never staunchly ideological—that is partly why everyone trusted him with the potential powers of the executive branch—so Millhiser's description of Washington as a firm proponent of "loose construction" stretches the truth.

Regardless, Millhiser's choice of characters is part of his problem. He picks two of the most ardent centralizers of the founding generation, Marshall and Hamilton, to prove his points. Yet, their comments on federal power during the months leading to ratification of the Constitution more closely resemble "tenther" arguments than Millhiser's. Hamilton said in 1788 that, "The most powerful obstacle to the members of Congress betraying the interest of their constituents, is the state legislatures themselves…jealous of federal encroachments, and armed with every power to check the first essays of treachery….Thus it appears that the very structure of the confederacy affords the surest preventatives from error, and the most powerful checks to misconduct." That sounds a lot like state interposition or "tentherism," doesn't it? And it was Hamilton who said that the direct democracy Millhiser advocates had historically produced "tyranny" and "deformity." So much for Hamilton being Millhiser's "guy." And Jefferson had this ringing endorsement of Hamilton: "Hamilton honest as a man, but, as a politician, believing in the necessity of either force or corruption to govern men."

What about Marshall? Marshall made the following statements during the Virginia Ratifying Convention of 1788: "Has the government of the United States the power to make laws on every subject?...Can they go beyond the delegated powers?...If they were to make a law not warranted by any of the powers enumerated, it would be considered by the judges as an infringement of the Constitution which they are to guard. They would not consider a law as coming under their jurisdiction. They would declare it void." He also thought a federal bill of rights was unnecessary because most States already had a bill of rights. In essence, the States protected their citizens from federal tyranny through the State courts. So, the federal government has "enumerated" and "delegated" powers and to go beyond those powers would violate the Constitution. Of course, Marshall thought those powers were expansive when he legislated from the bench during his time as Chief Justice, but in 1788 he argued a "State's rights" position. Millhiser left that part out, as do most Marshall supporters. It seems, however, that the Federalists Millhiser uses as "character witnesses" for his cause would not support his progressive agenda, regardless of how he tries to spin the issue.

And to make matters more interesting, perhaps the most ardent nationalist of the founding period, James Wilson of Pennsylvania, had this to say about the enumerated powers of the Constitution during the Pennsylvania ratifying convention of 1787:

> They found themselves embarrassed with another, of peculiar delicacy and importance. I mean that of drawing a proper line between the national government and the governments of the several states. It was easy to discover a proper and satisfactory principle on the subject. Whatever object of government is confined, in its operation and effects, within the bounds of a particular state, should be considered as belonging to the government of that state; whatever object of government extends, in its operation or effects, beyond the bounds of a particular state, should be considered as belonging to the government of the United States. But though this principle be sound and satisfactory, its application to particular cases would be accompanied with much difficult, because, in its application,

room must be allowed for great discretionary latitude of construction of the principle. In order to lessen or remove the difficulty arising from discretionary construction on this subject, an enumeration of particular instances, in which the application of the principle ought to take place, has been attempted with much industry and care. It is only a mathematical science that a line can be described with mathematical precision. But I flatter myself that, upon the strictest investigation, the enumeration will be found to be safe and unexceptionable, and accurate, too, in as great a degree as accuracy can be expected in a subject of this nature [emphasis added].

Later in the convention, Wilson declared that a small number of representatives in the federal government was adequate because "its objects are enumerated, and are not confined, in their causes or operations, to a county, or even to a single state. No one power is of such a nature as to require the minute knowledge of situations and circumstances necessary in state governments possessed of general legislative authority." To Wilson, enumerated meant limited, so members of the United States Congress had limited power under Article 1, Section 8. Surely, national health care and many other progressive measures require the "minute knowledge of situations and circumstances" in towns, counties, and even States and are not listed as enumerated powers of the federal government. In order to appease opponents of the Constitution, Wilson, a Federalist, rejected in 1787 an "elastic" interpretation of the "commerce clause," "general welfare clause," and "necessary and proper clause." Progressives like Millhiser won't discuss that.

Fallacy #3:
"Tentherism" Is "Dangerous" And "Authoritarian."

Millhiser is a lawyer by training, and it shows in his arguments against the Tenth Amendment. His piece reads like a legal brief in worthless American case law. He completely mischaracterizes Tenth Amendment supporters when he states, "Tenthers...want to strip the American people of their power to make such decisions and give it to a Supreme Court dominated by conservatives." Since when? As a principle, the Tenth Amendment movement does not care about the Supreme Court nor does it put its faith in Supreme Court decisions. The Tenth Amendment is about limited, self-government and the ability of the people of the States, those who elected members of the State ratifying conventions, those who elected the members of the State legislatures, and those who would take action under the Tenth Amendment, to check the power of the federal government through state interposition and decentralization, not case law. As Jefferson stated it is the right of "self-government" that directed the Kentucky Resolves, not centralization and "authoritarian" government, as Millhiser claims, and certainly not faith in the United States Supreme Court. Jefferson once said that he could not understand why people put faith in Supreme Court decisions because they were simply the "*obiter* dissertation of the Chief Justice [John Marshall]." So-called "tenthers" would agree.

I have pointed out before that decentralization is a philosophy that all groups, left or right, should support because it *protects* the interests of the community from oppressive centralization and authoritarian government. Certainly, Millhiser would agree that the people of California have a better idea of problems in California than the people of Alabama and vise-versa and for Alabama to legislate for California would be disastrous for the people of California. "Tenterism" is only dangerous to those who, like Millhiser, need a strong central authority to ram their agenda down the throats of the American people.

If Millhiser was truly interested in democracy, he would support the Tenth Amendment. Without question, many "Anti-federalists" who pushed for a State sovereignty amendment generally championed "democracy" and argued against ratifying the Constitution because they said it was undemocratic. By design, local and State governments are more democratic than the federal government as most have a more reasonable representative ratio, greater minority representation, and the direct democracy methods of initiate, referendum and recall. But that is not what Millhiser means by "democracy." His "democracy" is more akin to the national socialism of democratically elected progressives like Adolf Hitler, Benito Mussolini, and Francisco Franco, and it rests on the destruction of the limited federal republic of the Founders and the use of propaganda and demagoguery to influence voters. It is centralized power, or what John Randolph of Roanoke called the problem of "King Numbers," the tyranny of the fifty plus one percent. As many "Anti-federalists" pointed out in 1787 and 1788, Millhiser's brand of democracy cannot work over a large geographic and demographic community without destroying liberty.

Millhiser's conclusion that "Democracy is not easy..." reminded me of a line from the film *Green Zone*. During a briefing on the political instability of Iraq, administration official Clark Poundstone, played by Greg Kinnear, defended the dismantling of Iraq and ensuing violence and unrest upon the premise that "Democracy is messy!" See, progressives do think alike! Take our democracy and like it you ignorant wretches! Which is more authoritarian, a cause that champions individual and community liberty or one that forces people to think and act a certain way in the name of "progress?" I'll take my chances with the former.

A Neo-Impressionist Jefferson Portrait

THOMAS JEFFERSON WAS A RADICAL. He was also a conservative. His life represented a series of seemingly unorganized contradictions. He rooted his political philosophy in a consistent defense of federalism, an idea older than the British North American colonies. He was an American aristocrat who held opinions of society and man consistent with most of the prevailing racial and social attitudes of his day. Yet, Jefferson also sought to reform Virginia—his country—and tear down the established religious and educational hierarchy that had remained static for nearly two hundred years, a class system that while undemocratic produced most of the greatest statesmen of the founding generation. Jefferson thought his vision of republicanism would help advance the natural aristocracy and eliminate the pitfalls of ancient hereditary order, even an order that brought him to prominence.

That Jefferson can be many things makes him both more endearing and problematic for modern American society. Kevin Gutzman's *Thomas Jefferson— Revolutionary* attempts to bring these competing visions of Jefferson into focus. As Gutzman writes, "if he [Jefferson] had been a pointillist painter, there would be enough dots on his canvas for the viewer to be able to make out a clear image." For Gutzman, that neo-impressionist Jefferson is a consistent advocate of a political and social philosophy that can be traced to his days as a student at William and Mary. Jefferson's principles never wavered. That alone speaks volumes about the man.

Gutzman contends that every political rumination that passed Jefferson's lips should be viewed through the lens of federalism. "The principle of decentralization," Gutzman asserts, "always struck Jefferson as essential to popular government…" and "Whether in the highest federal offices or as a private citizen, he held the federal government to this principle until his very end." Indeed, Gutzman dedicates nearly one-third of the book to this important topic, though the other issues he discusses—religious liberty, "assimilation," "colonization," and education—were also undergirded by Jefferson's eye-level gaze with his mountains. Jefferson's work in codifying religious liberty never expanded beyond Virginia, and his effort to establish a university to rid Virginians of the "dark Federalist mills" of the North was a component of his greater concern for a complete revision of Virginia's educational system. But only in Virginia. Jefferson never believed he had a mandate to interfere with the local concerns of New England.

Gutzman spills a great deal of ink explaining how Jefferson's 1774 "A Summary View of the Rights of British America" outlined his general political philosophy. To Jefferson, the colonies had always been the masters of their own domain. This, in turn, relegated the Parliament and king to external concerns of defense and international trade. Jefferson wove that belief in local self-government into the Declaration of Independence and his many statements on the proper role of the general government vis-à-vis the States. While most historians have considered Jefferson's Kentucky Resolutions of 1798 to be a defense of free speech and the press, Gutzman argues that Jefferson intended that effort to be a defense of federalism. After all, he opened with an explanation of the Tenth Amendment to the Constitution. The regulation and punishment of speech and press were powers reserved to the people of the States, not the general government.

Gutzman's crisp writing buttresses this forcefully argued tome. His work is not intended to be a complete biography but a thorough sketch of the mind of perhaps the most misunderstood member of the founding generation. Gutzman aptly shows that the American tradition would be nothing without Jefferson, but more than anything, he has rescued and revitalized Jefferson's resolute defense of federalism. That alone is worth the price of the book.

Amendment IX

THE ENUMERATION IN THE CONSTITUTION, of certain rights, shall not be construed to deny or disparage others retained by the people.

In the waning days of the Philadelphia Convention in 1787, George Mason of Virginia, Elbridge Gerry of Massachusetts and Luther Martin of Maryland began pressing for the addition of a comprehensive bill of rights to the final draft of the Constitution. Roger Sherman of Connecticut immediately rejected their plea. A bill of rights, he said, was unnecessary because "The State Declarations of Rights are not repealed by this Constitution; and being in force are sufficient...." Sherman, a man who Thomas Jefferson regarded as one of the finest statesmen of the founding generation, reasoned that because the Constitution was mute on civil liberties and because it was a document with delegated and enumerated powers for the general purposes of the Union—the States United—the general government could no more legislate on matters of trial by jury than it could on the minutia of state law. Gerry's proposal to form a committee to draft of a bill of rights was unanimously defeated (votes were by State), and as a result Mason said he would rather cut off his right hand than sign the document. This exchange began the process for codifying the language of the Ninth Amendment.

During the ratifying process in the State conventions, several leading proponents of the document made arguments against a bill of rights that mirrored those Sherman gave in the Philadelphia Convention. James Wilson of Pennsylvania, perhaps the most ardent nationalist among the founding generation, said in the Pennsylvania Ratifying Convention that "A bill of rights annexed to a constitution is *an enumeration of the powers* reserved. If we attempt an enumeration, everything that is not enumerated is presumed to be given. The consequence is, that an imperfect enumeration would throw all implied power into the scale of the government, and the rights of the people would be rendered incomplete."

Alexander Hamilton of New York, the most famous nationalist of the founding period, echoed Wilson in *Federalist No. 84*. Adding a bill of rights, he said, "would contain various exceptions to powers which are not granted; and on this very account, would afford a colourable pretext to claim more than were granted. For why declare that things shall not be done which there is no power to do?" Both Hamilton and Wilson contended that a bill of rights would *destroy* liberty rather than protect it by allowing scheming men to enlarge the power of the central authority. In short, if a particular liberty was not protected by the list of rights, they believed it could be assumed that the government had the power to abridge that liberty. And, since all powers delegated to the general government were enumerated in the Constitution, they wondered why open that Pandora's Box?

Thus, the modern Ninth Amendment was born. As proposals for a bill of rights flooded into James Madison's hands in the months after the Constitution was ratified, he quickly realized that individuals needed assurances that their liberties would not be circumscribed by the Constitution nor would they be left to flutter in the wind should ambitious men usurp power from the States or the people. The Tenth Amendment protects the States and most importantly the federal compact among the States. The Ninth does the same for the people individually by implicitly recognizing the validity—and to the founding generation supremacy—of the several State declarations of rights. It is an enhancer. The original preamble to the Bill of Rights expressly stated that they were "restricting clauses" on the general government only. The Ninth Amendment ensured that the powers of the general government as operating on individuals would be further checked by the States. State declaration of rights often tended to be more detailed and comprehensive and therefore served as a more effective shield for the people.

Madison said in 1789 that Hamilton's argument against the Bill of Rights was "one of the most plausible…I have ever heard against the admission of a bill of rights into this system; but, I conceive, that it may be guarded against." He was referring to the Ninth Amendment. Of course, the powers of the general government in the modern era have spiraled out of control and today the two most ignored Amendments in the Bill of Rights are the Ninth and Tenth, arguably the most important Amendments to the founding generation. The States have always stood at the vanguard of individual liberty.

American citizens should remember that their first line of defense against both the State *and* Federal government rests in their separate *State* bill of rights. The founding generation believed that those declared rights coupled with the Ninth Amendment would prevent the modern leviathan in Washington D.C. We need to protect their legacy.

The Articles of Confederation

IF JAY LENO WERE to conduct a "Man on the Street" segment and ask random Americans to name the first constitution for the United States, the answers would probably range from, "The Declaration of Independence," to "the Preamble," to "Who cares?" The answer, of course, is The Articles of Confederation and Perpetual Union. American ignorance of the Articles is problematic for several reasons, not the least of which being a lack of understanding about the fundamental structure of the American general government. The Articles of Confederation is, in fact, the most maligned and misunderstood document in American political history. It is the bedrock of the United States Constitution which replaced it, and the Founders' conception of Union and the appropriate powers of government can be found in its Thirteen Articles.

The Articles of Confederation, principally authored by John Dickinson of Delaware, was formally ratified by the States in 1781, though both Dickinson and Benjamin Franklin had drafts in 1776 shortly after the States declared their independence from Great Britain. The central government–or general government as the founding generation called it–did not have an executive or judicial branch under the Articles, and the Congress did not have the power to tax or create a standing army. It could appropriate and borrow money, regulate trade, and make treaties, but the States could ignore these treaties, and the Congress did not have the power to regulate interstate trade. If the Congress needed money or troops, it had to make formal requests to the States and those would often be ignored, though perhaps not maliciously. The States were strapped financially themselves and often did not have the resources to cover the cost of two governments. Any legislation required a two-thirds majority to pass, making new laws difficult to enact. Most important, the general government could not coerce the States into obedience.

Each State had equal representation and could send between two and seven representatives. John Adams called them "ambassadors" of the States, meaning that the founding generation viewed the central government as little more than a pseudo united nations.

Often, Congress did not have a quorum, particularly in the months when the Congress met at Annapolis, Maryland. Northerners complained it was too hot and unsanitary and Southern culture (liquor drenched galas and balls) too decadent. Proponents of constitutional reform called the central government weak and ineffective.

Yet, the Constitution retained much of the character of the Articles of Confederation. The word "federal," as in the government established by the United States Constitution in 1788, and "confederation" carried the same meaning in the eighteenth-century. In fact, both Alexander Hamilton and James Madison called the general government under the Constitution a "confederation" in the *Federalist* essays. The Union was a league of States both during the Articles of Confederation and after the Constitution was ratified in 1788. It became "more perfect," but the nature of the Union itself was unaltered. It was and still is a Union of States–a federal Union or confederation–and as both the text of the Articles and the 10th Amendment to the Constitution make clear, the States retain all powers not delegated to the central government. The Articles included the qualifying word "expressly" in Article 2, and there was an attempt to include the same qualifier in what became the 10th Amendment to the Constitution, but it was deemed redundant. Expressly was implied by both the Preamble to the Bill of Rights and the language of the Amendment itself.

Much of the wording of the Constitution was lifted directly from the Articles as well and carries the same meaning. The now infamous "general welfare clause" of the Constitution can be found in Article 3 and Article 8 of the Articles of Confederation. As Roger Sherman explained in the Philadelphia Convention in 1787, the "general welfare" was defined as "defense against foreign danger… against internal disputes and a resort to force…treaties with foreign nations… regulating foreign commerce and drawing revenue from it….*All other matters, civil and criminal, would be much better in the hands of the states* [emphasis added]." Sherman added the clause to the Constitution, so his understanding has merit. The "general welfare" was for the Union, not individuals, and because both the Articles and the Constitution act on the States (the "them" in both documents) and not individuals, the meaning did not change from one document to the next. The same can be said for the "privileges and immunities" and the "full faith and credit" clauses of the Constitution. Both are found in Article 4 of the Articles of Confederation. There are others, but these are the most cited of the document.

The Articles of Confederation

The Articles of Confederation was the first Constitution for the United States. The name of the Union, "The United States of America," is found in Article 1 of the Articles of Confederation and the general temper of the Articles carried forward to the Preamble of the United States Constitution. Article 3 of the Articles and the Preamble are similar in both language and tone. When the Constitution was ratified in 1788, the *proponents* of the document insisted that nothing changed in regard to the *federal* nature of the government. The Union was not altered, the government had not been consolidated, and the States still retained all powers not enumerated in the Constitution, just as in the Articles of Confederation. Constitutional scholars would do well to read the Articles in conjunction with the Constitution. Certainly, the Constitution strengthened the powers of the general government, and astute opponents of the Constitution warned that these powers would ultimately be abused, but the Constitution was sold to and understood by the States in 1788 to be little more than an amended form of the Union established by the Articles in 1783. If that is the case, then the Articles should not be ignored or denigrated, but studied as the foundation of the general government of the United States, both in principle and spirit.

Judicial Power: The Founders' Design

WITH THE CONFIRMATION HEARINGS of Sonia Sotomayor, the Supreme Court has again taken center stage in American politics. We have heard about her "wise Latina" comment and her positions on abortion and gay marriage, and it seems that these are the central issues in the debate; however, the question the Senate Judiciary Committee should be asking is would Sotomayor, as a member of the Supreme Court, follow the guidelines established by the founding generation in relation to court power? If not, and it is obvious she will be confirmed, what can Americans do about a court bent on "legislating from the bench?" It seems Americans need a little history lesson about the original intent of the Supreme Court.

The idea of an "elastic" Constitution and "legislating from the bench" originated in the founding generation. The disheveled and lazy socialite, John Marshall of Virginia, provided the intellectual basis of judicial activism when, in the 1803 *Marbury v. Madison* decision as Chief Justice of the Supreme Court, he lectured President Thomas Jefferson on Supreme Court jurisdiction. Marshall stated that "it is emphatically the province and duty of the judicial department to say what the law is" and ultimately decide on the constitutionality of legislation.

What most Americans don't realize is that "Judicial review," as it has since been called, is not an enumerated power of the Supreme Court. You won't find those words in the Constitution. Certainly, many members of the founding generation believed the Court would, as a co-equal branch of government, ultimately be able to check legislative and executive authority through its appellate jurisdiction, but that pertained only to *federal* law. Marshall himself argued during the 1788 Virginia Ratifying Convention that the Supreme Court could only rule on federal law, not state statutes. This was an attempt to appease Anti-Federalists who warned that the Supreme Court would run roughshod over civil liberties and the other branches of government. Marshall, of course, was being disingenuous. Many of his later rulings smacked down state sovereignty and enlarged the power of the Supreme Court. But Marshall was the exception rather than the rule in the founding generation in relation to the interpretation of Supreme Court powers. The members of his Court certainly agreed with him, but not everyone was convinced.

Jefferson wrote later in life that the "judicial review" was simply the opinion of John Marshall, and not the original intent of the framers of the Constitution. In fact, he said in 1815 that, "The question whether the judges are invested with exclusive authority to decide on the constitutionality of a law has been heretofore a subject of consideration with me in the exercise of official duties. Certainly, there is not a word in the Constitution which has given that power to them more than to the Executive or Legislative branches." In 1798, Jefferson and his lieutenant James Madison secretly authored the Virginia and Kentucky Resolves to protest the unconstitutional Sedition Act of 1798. These resolves outlined the doctrine of state interposition, better known as nullification. In essence, the states, acting in their sovereign capacity, could declare a federal law unconstitutional and refuse to adhere to its provisions. This was certainly a measure of last resort, but Northern members of the founding generation believed in it enough to invoke nullification during the 1815 Hartford Convention, a protest of the War of 1812 and the Madison administration. Nullification worked in 1798 but with the end of the War of 1812, Northern Federalist participants in the Hartford Convention were discredited, called unpatriotic, and for a time, disappeared as a political force. Still, the question of "judicial review" appeared unsettled.

Of course, the Constitution provided a way to rid the American polity of aggressive judges. Federal judicial appointees are subject to impeachment, and the Republicans who controlled the Congress in 1804 tried to make an example of Supreme Court Justice Samuel Chase. The House of Representatives impeached him for partisan political attacks from the bench, but the Senate found him not guilty. Before the final verdict, Marshall was genuinely scared that he would be next on the chopping block, but once it became clear that the power of impeachment would be stripped of its teeth, the Marshall court went on a political rampage for the next thirty years. Jefferson again said that he thought both houses of Congress should simply remove the whole bunch. George Washington thought that only unconstitutional legislation should be subject to an executive veto. In other words, both men agreed that each branch of government should act as a check on the other.

Unfortunately, Congress has lost the will to attack the judicial branch, the president uses the veto as a legislative hammer rather than a simple check on the legislative branch, and the people of the states have lost their understanding of their own political power and the ultimate sovereignty of the states. Either the states or the Congress could, and should, check the federal court system, but this will take a concerted effort to re-educate Americans about the original intent of the Constitution and judicial power. If enough Americans read the warnings of the Anti-Federalists during the state ratification conventions of 1788, it should become clear that the men who ratified the Constitution had a different, and much more limited, interpretation of Supreme Court jurisdiction than the modern members of the bench. Sotomayor will not change the ideological composition of the Court, but that should not matter. Judicial review was an *obiter dictum* of John Marshall that has since become an accepted practice. Returning to the original intent of the majority of the founding generation would, in many ways, make Sotomayor's political ideology irrelevant. Judicial review would be a thing of the past, particularly in relation to federal control of the states, and the court would remain a co-equal, rather than a dominant branch of the federal government.

CHEESEHEAD SECESSIONISTS

IN APRIL, SEVERAL MEMBERS of the Wisconsin Republican Party inserted a resolution in the State Party platform expressly recognizing the right of their State to secede from the Union. It was voted down May 3, but the move received national press. The Daily Beast published an article on both the resolution and modern secession movements in Vermont and Alaska, and the Drudge Report included a link to the story.

Predictably the resolution drew critics. A little-known Democratic candidate for governor donned a make-shift Confederate uniform and canvassed the convention trying to get someone—anyone—to talk to him, particularly the media. Don't we all know that secession is simply a code-word (a "dog whistle" as the moronic Left likes to say) for slavery and racism? He personifies American stupidity. Even cheeseheads who support limited government threw the idea under the bus. "No, sir," they say, "I don't support an idea that might actually rid our people of Washington oversight, heavy handed one-size fits all policies, or unconstitutional usurpation of power. I want to work within the system to affect change." That plan has worked well so far, hasn't it?

Americans from cradle to grave are told that secession is treason and un-American and has only been threatened or used to justify horrendous human rights abuses. I might agree if Massachusetts had pulled it off in 1803 or 1815 like they intended. Who would want to live under their brand of Puritanical nonsense?

One hit piece on the proposal in the *Milwaukee Journal Sentinel* focused on the resolution's author, Michael Murphy, the 41-year-old leader of the libertarian wing of the State Party, and by default yours truly. Murphy embedded a video on his website I did with Tom Woods on the legality of secession and cited the video as clear proof that his position is legitimate. According, however, to the esteemed "journalist" who wrote the *Sentinel* piece, my talks before the SCV and my articles critical of Lincoln invalidates my position. He obviously failed logic 101. The piece is classic ad hominem rubbish. The "journalist" cannot refute the idea of secession and does not understand the constitutional or legal underpinnings, so he attempts a character assassination. It would be funny if not so common among the media and the modern political class. If you can't disprove the ideas of your opponents, call them names. It worked in kindergarten.

Murphy correctly points out that the idea has never been refuted intellectually or legally, only by bullets. The "journalist" calls this stance "completely outrageous." Murphy committed a mortal sin and he must now answer to the high priests of nationalism, i.e. the political class and their media minions. His penance is ostracism from the Republican Party and ridicule from the gatekeepers of undeniable truth. Ignorance is strength.

There is, however, a sliver-lining to this exchange. We are starting to win. In the aftermath of 1865, no one would have attempted to insert a secession resolution (innocuous as it was) into a State Party platform, particularly in Wisconsin, the birthplace of Lincoln's Republican Party. That is until now. Secession was bloodied and bludgeoned on the battlefield, but it is the American tradition, codified by Jefferson's Declaration of Independence and pursued in both the North and South several times before the War in 1861. The rise of secessionist groups in the United States in the last twenty years is clear proof that the Lincoln myth of perpetual Union and forced association is fading, albeit slowly.

Young people have seen that the emperor has no clothes and are flocking to the principles of independence in growing numbers, both personally and politically. And it is peaceful. There are Michael Murphys in every State. Our job is to cultivate them, to help them understand that the Southern political tradition of Washington, Jefferson, Taylor, Henry, Calhoun, Lee, Davis, and Bledsoe did not die after Appomattox. It lives in the spirit of liberty, of independence, and most importantly, of truth.

National Democratic Party (NDP)

9 JULY 1896. WILLIAM JENNINGS BRYAN, the young, free-silver proponent from Nebraska had just finished his vitriolic assault on the gold standard at the Democratic Convention in Chicago, Illinois by raising the applause to a fever pitch with the following iconic line: "Having behind us the producing masses of this nation and the world, supported by the commercial interests, the laboring interests, and the toilers everywhere, we will answer their demand for a gold standard by saying to them: You shall not press down upon the brow of labor this crown of thorns, you shall not crucify mankind upon a cross of gold."

He was carried around the room on the shoulders of the cheering delegates, and two days later accepted the nomination to serve as the presidential candidate for the Democratic Party. But not every Democrat rejoiced. While Bryan's "Cross of Gold" speech has been labeled one of the most important political statements in American history, many in his own party thought Bryan had subverted "Democratic principles" by playing fast and loose with the facts and by pandering to the masses. A famous political cartoon in *Judge* Magazine depicted Bryan as a snake swallowing the Democratic Party whole.

In response, several prominent Democrats, including President Grover Cleveland, supported the creation of a splinter party in order to give Democrats an avenue to avoid voting Republican. Led by members from the Cleveland cabinet and the United States Congress, the group met in Indianapolis in September 1896 and selected John M. Palmer, a former Union general and United States Senator from Illinois, as its presidential nominee, and Simon B. Buckner, a former Confederate general and ex-governor of Kentucky, as its vice-presidential candidate. This event is now regarded as little more than a footnote in American political history, but modern Americans, particularly libertarians and paleo-conservatives, should take note of the party, its history, and its platform.

Politics since the 1850s had become a game of sectional division. The Republican Party was based on sectional animosity and when the Democratic Party split in 1860, some Northern Democrats uncomfortable with secession found a home with the Republicans until after the war. The Northern "Peace Democrats" stayed true to the traditional principles of the party: free trade, sound money, limited government, and Constitutional law, but they were outnumbered and marginalized in much of the North by the rabid Republican "reptiles" as one Democrat called them. It seems that those who favor limited government are always pushed to the back burner during times of "crisis."

Reconstruction altered the American political landscape. Men who considered military Reconstruction an abomination defected in droves to the Democratic Party, and as the South regained its political footing, the Party reclaimed its national flavor. The stolen presidential election of 1876 illustrated that a strong Democratic candidate with national appeal could compete against the Yankee dominated Republican Party. Democrats celebrated victory in 1884 when former New York Governor Grover Cleveland defeated Maine Radical Republican James G. Blaine in a close, mud-slinging contest for president.

Democrats had regained power, but continued success appeared elusive. Cleveland lost in 1888 due to voter fraud but returned to the executive mansion in 1892; however, because of the Panic of 1893, the Party seemed to be losing favor among the American public, particularly in the South and West. Cleveland's support for a sound money policy that maintained the gold standard and fiscal responsibility produced cracks in the party. Several Democrats began pushing for inflationary bimetallism and the free coinage of silver, and they found support among farmers and debtors theoretically hurt by the deflationary boom of the 1880s and 1890s. Never mind that the Sherman Silver Purchase Act of 1890 – authored by the "Old Icicle," Republican John Sherman of Ohio, brother of General William T. Sherman – had caused a run on gold and a currency crisis. To them, silver seemed to be the inflationary tonic to their economic troubles. More money in circulation meant a better economy, right? Well, at least it meant potentially more votes.

Of course, the newly created National Democratic Party (NDP) responded with a resolute NO! The executive committee of the NDP published a "Campaign Text-Book" to provide facts and arguments and was "intended for writers – especially for editors; and for speakers – particularly those engaged in debate; and it is put in handy form that it may be carried in the pocket and easily consulted."

This little handbook is a treasure of information and a valuable window into the 1896 campaign and late-nineteenth-century politics.

The NDP emphasized that it was the only national party left. By continuing to insist on a protective tariff and illegal taxation, Republicans could not count on many votes in the South or West, and the Bryan silverites alienated Northern and Eastern sound money proponents. A platform that adhered to the gold standard and limited, Constitutional government would find support among all sections and people. This, coupled with the nomination of a "Union/Confederate" ticket showed that the NDP was willing to put sectional and class division aside for the good of the United States. Too bad not many listened.

The handbook characterized a true Democrat as one who believed "in the ability of every individual, unassisted, if unfettered by law, to achieve his own happiness, and, therefore, that to every citizen there should be secured the right and opportunity peaceably to pursue whatever course of conduct he would, provided such conduct deprived no other individual of the equal freedom of the same right and opportunity." In short, true Democrats believed in "Individual Liberty" and "disbelieved in the ability of government, through paternal legislation or supervision, to increase the happiness of the nation." To that end, the party proclaimed it was "opposed to paternalism and all class legislation." This, of course, is part of the American political tradition, a tradition that has been co-opted by the left in an attempt to portray "equality" and "justice for all" through government aid as the foundation of the United States. The NDP could see the writing on the wall in 1896. Anyone with a brain could. Free silver was just the start.

Buckner connected the dots in his acceptance speech. He insisted "that for everyone hundred cents' worth of work done by the laborer he shall receive one hundred cents" and called for "the commerce of the world shall be brought to our ports in free ships, untaxed for the benefit of any special interest in this country." Buckner declared that the free-silver platform championed by Bryan and adopted by the Democrats at Chicago was a ruse and a trap. They were not and could not be called traditional Democrats. Rather, they were a ship flying the false colors of Republican "protection and fiatism and Populistic communism, repudiation, and anarchism..." in the hope that they would lull the unsuspecting American public into their clutches and then bury them "in the chasm which they dig for the prosperity of the country." Gold, fiscal responsibility, and individual liberty were the only hallmarks of good government.

Most Americans forget or were never told that the Republican Party passed the first income tax in American history and that it used "greenbacks" to inflate the money supply during the War for Southern Independence in order to pay for the military conquest of the South. Republicans supported the fusion of government, finance, and industry, i.e. state capitalism, and central banking. The NDP correctly illustrated that the Republican Party was still the party of taxes in 1896. (It still is; they just don't tell you that.) The Republican candidate for president in that year, William McKinley, authored the bill that provided for the highest protective tariff in American history, the McKinley Tariff of 1890. This taxed imported goods at a rate of forty-six percent, a rate that certainly prohibited free commerce and in part led to the Panic of 1893.

The Republicans did support the gold standard, and they used that to their advantage in 1896 by running with the issue during the election. Many "gold Democrats" supported McKinley because of that one issue in both 1896 and 1900 and only defected in 1904 when Alton Parker was nominated by the Democrats on a sound money platform. The "gold Democrats" were finally smothered by the election of Woodrow Wilson in 1912, the man who at one time backed the NDP only to become one of the most ardent centralizers in American history.

The creation of the NDP was a last gasp effort to save the founding principles of the United States. No major party has adhered to them since. They tallied weak numbers during the 1896 election (less than 1 percent of the total popular vote) and only finished ahead of the Prohibition Party candidate by seven thousand votes. The Party posted fairly good numbers in the Northeast, and in Delaware and Alabama, but not enough to swing any of those states. These small numbers have led to the conclusion that they were irrelevant dinosaurs of the late-nineteenth century. Not so fast.

The NDP proved that there were still men of importance who favored limited government, state's rights, fiscal responsibility, and the individual, and though few of them voted for the Palmer/Buckner ticket, sound money and limited government remained important political issues until Franklin Roosevelt pulled the United States off a hard money policy in 1934 and usurped legislative powers through the New Deal. Excessive federal spending on both wars and social engineering programs ultimately led the United States to abandon sound money entirely under Richard Nixon. That, as Paul Harvey used to say, is the rest of the story, but it doesn't have to be.

Americans are beginning to relearn the benefits of a sound money policy, and the principles of the NDP have not disappeared from the American polity. The Party "text-book" could still be used today as a general handbook of limited government and sound money. Most of the book is dedicated to a defense of the gold standard and a "myth busting" attack on free silver proponents and inflationary zealots. In one particularly interesting section, the NDP illustrates how falling agricultural prices had nothing to do with the gold standard and how an inflated money supply would neither raise wholesale prices nor bring prosperity. As production and efficiency increase, prices will naturally decrease relative to the value of the dollar. Inflation would not solve that economic reality.

As the NDP stated, "What the working man wants is a dollar whose purchasing power either remains unchanged or increases." Keynesian economics and the FED won't provide a stable and powerful dollar – 100 cents for every 100 cents of work. Only limited government and gold can do that. Americans may not have the NDP or "gold Democrats," but we have their handbook, freedom of speech, and the Internet, the only items needed to disseminate the truth. The pendulum may finally be swinging back the other way.

Part II:
Lincolnites, Neoconservatives, and Progressives

Democracy, Liberty, Equality: Lincoln's American Revolution

SEVERAL MONTHS AGO, *The American Conservative* magazine reviewed *Forgotten Conservatives in American History*, a book I co-authored with Clyde Wilson, and one reader left an online comment about the book. Normally, I do not discuss responses to reviews, but this one caught my eye, in particular because the reader admits that they know little about conservatism yet think they are qualified to discuss conservatism. The reader said:

> "I have a hard time accepting many of the people noted in the review are real conservatives, in the Burkean sense. My take on Burke, whose ideas I only know from cursory reading, is that he would have been appalled by the South choosing secession, or war, as several of the author's – and the reviewer – choices advocated. In addition, the authors' bent towards Southern Civil War arguments on State's Rights reveals a thorough misunderstanding of the volatile and varied arguments that occurred throughout the 13 states during the development of the Constitution."

This quote metis a response for two reasons: 1) As she admits, she has little understanding of Burke, and I believe that the American Burke, John Randolph of Roanoke, would have advanced secession in 1861 and would have recoiled at the revolutionary changes taking place in America in during that time—he already had just a generation before, and 2) the "thorough misunderstanding" I supposedly have about the Constitution reveals that Americans fundamentally believe Lincoln's "democratic conservative" rhetoric both before and during the

War. Most see him as the messiah of American political religion rather than the antichrist, the bridge rather than the chasm between the 1860s and the founding generation. That must change.

In August 1863, eight months after Abraham Lincoln's constitutionally dubious Emancipation Proclamation took effect, Giuseppe Garibaldi, the famous Italian egalitarian nationalist, congratulated Lincoln in a fawning letter, writing: "Posterity will call you the great emancipator, a more enviable title than any crown could be, and greater than any merely mundane treasure." Giuseppe Mazzini, Garibaldi's Leftist revolutionary mentor and ally, called Lincoln the "benefactor of mankind" and ardently supported the Union cause after the Proclamation. In the United States, Elizabeth Cady Stanton and her allies in the women's suffragist movement formed the Women's Loyal League, an organization that Stanton said "voiced the solemn lessons of the war: Liberty to all; national protection for every citizen under our flag; universal suffrage, and universal amnesty." The League resolved that, "There can never be a true peace in this Republic until the civil and political rights of all citizens are established."

Charles Sumner, the Massachusetts Senator who suffered humiliation at the cane of South Carolinian Preston Brooks, declared in 1862 that the Southern States "ceased to exist," even if they should return to the Union. He reasoned that this was the only way to secure universal political and civil rights for all Americans regardless of race, and while he later balked at Stanton's pressuring to expand the Fourteenth Amendment to include women, Thaddeus Stevens, the "Great Commoner," embraced the cause. Stevens is a fine example of the "Jacobin" revolutionary spirit during the War. At one time, most historians categorized and described the leaders of the "radical" wing of the Republican Party as "Jacobins." That has since changed (witness the way Thad and his ilk were portrayed in Speilberg's *Lincoln*) and while the radical Republicans attempted to distance themselves from that term, it was no stretch to call them that. Stevens, in fact, was their greatest crusader. His war was to "punish the South" and "remake the South," but more importantly to remake the United States as a whole. He supported all reform causes expect temperance and pseudo-bourgeois moral righteousness restrictions on foul language. Stevens was alone here. Nearly every radical Republican favored prohibition. Theirs was a Puritanical crusade against both private and public immorality.

Others with nearly as high a profile gladly championed Jacobin reform. As historian Fawn Brodie noted, Horace Greely, the famed newspaperman from New York and later presidential candidate, favored "prohibition, women's rights, the abolition of sweatshops, free homesteads, and Brook Farm socialism." The Massachusetts radical Wendell Phillips ran for governor on a reform platform in

1870 that championed "the overthrow of monopolies, the abolition of the privileged classes, universal education...obliteration of poverty...a ten-hour day for factory work and eight hours hereafter," and equal pay for women. Nearly all opposed capital punishment (except for treasonous Southerners, of course, as radical Benjamin Wade wanted to execute Confederate leaders) and nearly all supported reform of the penal code. Samuel Chase, as Chief Justice of the Supreme Court, favored the abolition of the death penalty in all cases except "willful murder." One historian wrote that, "Their story is the story of American progress," and each "brought to Washington firmly held ideas of social betterment."

Clearly, to Stanton, Sumner, Stevens, Chase, Greeley, and even international observers, the War was a revolution, in the same spirit as that which swept France in 1789 and all of Europe in 1848. Abolition was just one component of a comprehensive movement to remake America into a Northern ideologically dominated Puritanical Utopia. But they were not the majority in the Republican Party in 1860, so how did their War become the War? The link is Abraham Lincoln and "American democracy."

The distinguished historian Frederick Jackson Turner wrote in his monumental work *The Frontier in American History*:

> If the later West offers few such striking illustrations of the relation of the wilderness to idealistic schemes, and if some of the designs were fantastic and abortive, none the less the influence is a fact. Hardly a Western State but has been the Mecca of some sect or band of social reformers, anxious to put into practice their ideals, in vacant land, far removed from the checks of a settled form of social organization....[and] The democracy of the West is deeply affected by the ideals brought by [German and Scandinavian] immigrants from the Old World. To them America was not simply a new home; it was a land of opportunity, of freedom, of democracy. It meant to them, as to the American pioneer that preceded them, the opportunity to destroy the bonds of social caste that bound them in their older home, to hew out for themselves in a new country a destiny proportioned to the powers that God had given them....

Turner viewed Lincoln as a continuation of the American frontier ideal, a conservationist of the ancient democratic order of the American experience brought forward by the American War for Independence. While the Jacobins viewed Lincoln as too cautious, a drag on their Utopian designs, he was, nevertheless, a closet admirer of their zeal and morality. The Jacobins called Lincoln a conservative—as have nearly every American historian since—and in a unique twist, Turner concluded that Lincoln displayed a uniquely American conservatism, one that is more recognizable to Louis Hartz than Mel Bradford or Russell Kirk. Lincoln, Turner said, was a defender of the American principles of democracy against the ruinous doctrines of oligarchy and the ancien regime. Turner believed that the spirit of the West produced Thomas Jefferson (a Southerner), the Declaration of Independence, Andrew Jackson (a Southerner)— who "broke down the traditions of conservative rule...and opened the temple of the nation to the populace"—and Abraham Lincoln. "Best of all," he wrote, "the West gave, not only to the American, but to the unhappy and oppressed of all lands, a vision of hope, and assurance that the world held a place where were to be found high faith in man and the will and power to furnish him the opportunity to grow to the full measure of his own capacity....Let us see to it that the ideals of the pioneer in his log cabin shall enlarge into the spiritual life of a democracy where civic power shall dominate and utilize individual achievement for the common good."

Turner, of course, was simply caught up on Cult of Lincoln, a cult that Lincoln himself helped forge during his successful run for president in 1860 and his folksy, home-spun speeches aimed at equating democracy with reform and American founding principles with his—and ultimately those of the Jacobins'—policies. To a group of Germans in 1861, Lincoln said "I am for those means which will give the greatest good to the greatest number," and in a speech just two days later insisted that the "majority must rule" and the "voice of the people" must be the deciding factor as to "rights under the Constitution." In New Jersey in 1861, Lincoln attached his impending presidency with the "original idea for which [National Independence] was made." National Independence is his term. What was Lincoln's ideal? "Liberty, not alone to the people of this country, but hope to the world for all future time. It was that which gave promise that in due time the weights should be lifted from the shoulders of all men, and that all should have an equal chance. That is the sentiment embodied in that Declaration of Independence." Clever. This is why the Straussians attach their type of "Conservatism" to the Declaration, because Lincoln did. And Lincoln's famous Gettysburg Address continued this theme by insisting that the "government of the people, by the people, and for the people" should not perish from this Earth. Lincoln also famously wrote, "As I would not be a slave, so I would not be a master." Yet, while Lincoln and other reformers were insisting (incorrectly) that their cause was one of continuity with the founding principles, other Americans, both North and South, contemporary and predecessor, saw the War and the history of America in a different light.

In 1829, John Randolph of Roanoke, the American version of Edmund Burke, made a speech at the Virginia Constitutional Convention typically titled

"King Numbers." He was attempting to thwart proposals made by western county representatives to make the Virginia constitution more democratic. His ruminations on democracy can only be described as prophetic, particularly when compared to the a-historical nature of Lincoln's appeal to a "democratic" America and the Jacobin preference for reform, what Randolph called "innovation." And, it must be noted that Randolph requested to be buried standing up and facing west in order to keep his eye on Henry Clay, Lincoln's political mentor. That makes Randolph's assertions more sagacious.

Randolph considered democracy to be the bane of society, the final blow to good government, and he classified innovation and reform as the spawn of "obedience to the all-prevailing principle that vox populi, vox dei; aye, Sir, the all-prevailing principles that Numbers and Numbers alone, are to regulate all things in political society, in the very teeth of those abstract natural rights of man which constitute the only shadow of claim to exercise this monstrous tyranny." He worried aloud about the results of reform, for "I have by experience learned that changes, even in the ordinary law of the land, do not always operate as the drawer of the bill, or the Legislative body, may have anticipated; and of all the things in the world, a Government, whether ready made to suit casual customers or made per order, is the very last that operates as its framers intended. Governments are like revolutions: you may put them in motion, but I defy you to control them after they are in motion." And in a fearful flourish, one that generations of Americans, particularly those in 1861, should have rendered as predictive:

> Are we men…Or are we in truth, a Robinhood Society discussing rights in the abstract? Have we no house over our heads? Do we forget that we are living under a Constitution which has shielded us for more than half a century?—that we are not a parcel of naked and forlorn savages on the shores of New Holland; and that the worst that can come is that we shall live under the same Constitution that we have lived under, freely and happily, for half a century? To their monstrous claims of power, we plead this prescription; but then we are told: nullum tempus occurrit Regi (no time runs against the king). King whom? King Numbers. And they will not listen to a prescription of fifty-four years—a period greater by four years than would secure a title to the best estate in the Commonwealth, unsupported by any other shadow of right. Nay, Sir, in this case, prescription operates against possession. They tell us it is only a case of long-continued, and therefore of aggravated, injustice. They say to us, in words the most courteous and soft…"we shall be—we will be—we must be your masters, and you shall submit.

That should have served as enough warning for schemers, reformers, and innovators that such ideas were disastrous in the long term, yet to the Jacobins in Lincoln's party bent on revolution, the other side in the debate did not exist. Charles Sumner once slammed his fist on the table in an emphatic denial that any point other than his own had merit. His voice was not soft. The Jacobins intended to be heard. That is revolutionary fanaticism.

Northern Democrats during the War are often painted as dishonest partisans intent on whipping the flames of opposition through grand speeches laced with hyper-sensitive panic about Republican victory. These historians often focus on race—though not every Jacobin favored the quality of the races, nor did Lincoln himself—and they view the results of the war through their own progressive lenses. The war produced salutary effects in their mind, and therefore the Democrats had little to offer other than misguided paranoia. That would be an acceptable position if not for the biting truth of many of their statements.

Common soldiers often complained about what they viewed as a shift in war aims in 1862, particularly those who came from Democratic families. One Indiana soldier wrote that, "If emancipation is to be the policy of this war…I do not care how quick the country goes to pot." An officer from New York opined that if the war became a crusade for the "black Republicans" for "an abolition war…I for one shall be sorry that I ever lent a hand to it." Many men deserted rather than wage a revolutionary crusade of abstract human rights. The Union was one thing but fighting for reform was another. Yet, in fairness, as the historian James McPherson has noted, by 1864, the war had taken a revolutionary tone for many of the common soldiers in the North. Some still opposed the reformist agenda, but most (McPherson concludes probably 80 percent) thought emancipation should be a war aim. As one Michigan solider said, "After this war is over, this whole country will undergo a change for the better…Abolishing slavery will dignify labor; that fact of itself will revolutionize everything…." This was Lincoln's democratic army at work. Without the Union army vote, he would have been in trouble in the 1864 election. As in France, the Union levee en masse "revolutionized everything" with blood and steel.

Yet, astute thinkers in the North and South understood the score. Samuel S. Cox, a Democratic representative from Ohio, and firm Lincoln opponent, warned of the consequences of unchecked reform:

> Extreme men drag the moderate men with them. The devil, it is said, holds his own by a hair. He has entered into this majority as he entered into the swine; and they will, by diabolic impulse, be driven at last into the sea. At last—but when is that time to come? When the country is ruined?…They will not halt until

their darling schemes are consummated. History tells us that such zealots do not and cannot go backward. Robespierre, the gentle judge at Arras, in 1783, resigned rather than condemn a criminal to death. In ten years after, filled with the enthusiasm of Rousseau, he claimed for the blacks in the French colonies a participation in political rights, and exclaimed, not unlike members here, "Let the colonies perish, rather than a principle!" But he was the same Robespierre who led the Jacobins to demand the King's head in 1792, who established the reign of terror, and whose motto was, "that to live was a crime." He could take no step backward. Onward, onward from excess to excess, until his name became the obloquy of the world. Only his own death, lay the same terrorism, ended his terrible rule. The same result took place at Rome, in the time of Gracchus. It does so everywhere when passion is driven to excess. Our only safety now lies in moderate and patriotic counsels, not rash and vindictive action....

United States Senator James A. Bayard of Delaware frequently characterized the Republicans as Jacobins similar to those who initiated the Reign of Terror and that the war was one of extermination of the Southern people. He was most distressed over the "Puritans and Quakers" who ran the government both in Washington and Delaware. In 1862, he wrote that "I fear Lincoln will give us a more radical [cabinet], for Beecher declared the other day in Boston, that 'God was a radical and the devil a conservative.' What a clergyman!"

This charge against Northern Puritanical zeal was commonplace among critique of the Republicans in the South, both before and after the war. Reform was the centerpiece of their crusade, and while the perception exists that they never succumbed to the excesses of the revolution, over 300,000 Southerners who baptized their fields of revolution with blood would disagree. The Republicans did not guillotine Southern leaders, but they certainly emasculated the South and over time have transformed the nature of the federal republic. That is their legacy.

Writing one year after the conclusion of the war, the Southern newspaperman Edward Pollard wrote that in 1861 Abraham Lincoln "announced a great political discovery. It was that all former statesman of America had lived, and written, and labored under a great delusion; that the States, instead of having created the Union, were its creatures; that they obtained their sovereignty and independence from it, and never possessed either until the Convention of 1787." This, Pollard concluded, gave Lincoln the ability to woo America into a false religion of democracy, a democracy that led to disastrous war and striking political revolution, not in the South as he claimed, but in the North, a revolution he helped begin. Lincoln was the Duke of Orleans, the tragic figure who hoped to quell a revolutionary spirit only to meet his demise through assassination, the Duke by decapitation, Lincoln through a bullet. America, the founders' America, and the Constitution as ratified by that generation, were shredded by the Jacobin war machine.

Looking back, we can see the seeds being sewn long before 1861, but it was the zeal of the Jacobins that made it possible. Perhaps if Americans had listened to the founding generation, then the cruel war never would have happened. They understood that a Union must be for specific purposes and never consolidated. As Benjamin Randall of MASSACHUSETTS said in 1787, "if the states were consolidated…it would introduce manners among us which would set us at continual variance." The Jacobins took care of that by waging a war of revolution and extermination. Emancipation was but one component of a larger plan at consolidation and centralization with the ultimate objective being the recreation of the United States. Barack Obama has not been incorrect when he has suggested that his administration continues to remake America. That process has been ongoing for 150 years. We are living in the end result of Lincoln's American Revolution. Obama is simply wearing his red Republican kepi.

All Hail Abe!

TODAY WE CELEBRATE THE BIRTHDAY of the log cabin born, rough-hewn, rail-splitting, bare-knuckled, "pock-faced, stoop-shouldered, slab-sided assistant storekeeper," lewd, vulgar, uninspiring, "ordinary Western man" from Illinois, Abraham Lincoln.

Lincoln's life and image is a series of irreconcilable dichotomies:

He had no military experience worth noting—he waged war on wild onion fields during the Black Hawk War and cleaned up the dead following two battles—yet personally led the largest military effort in the history of the United States to that point, often sleeping in the War Department and personally appointing and replacing generals at will.

He had little education or understanding of American government and virtually no political experience yet is considered by most Americans to be the greatest statesman and political theorist in American history.

He had a profitable career as a highly paid attorney representing big business in Illinois and a fine home across from the capital in Springfield, yet Lincoln is portrayed as a successful "man of the people."

He is characterized as the heir to the Jeffersonian tradition, yet his stand against "State's Rights" and federalism is in sharp contrast to Jefferson's political philosophy of decentralization.

He called for 75,000 troops to put down a "rebellion" he instigated by telling Republicans not to compromise with the South in the months before the War (even having William H. Seward feign sick to avoid meeting with commissioners from South Carolina interested in settling pressing financial matters between the two governments) and by insisting on provisioning Fort Sumter when his leading military advisors warned that it would start a war, the "desired effect" as Lincoln later said, yet he is viewed today as the president reluctantly dragged into a war he did not want.

He had no declaration of war and by default, according to the Constitution, committed treason against the States, "waging war against them," yet Lincoln is often viewed as the man who saved the Constitution.

He insisted a government "of the people, by the people, and for the people" must not perish from the earth, and yet waged war against thirteen popularly elected State governments and one central government formed on the principle of self-determination.

He favored colonization of free blacks, never believed in racial equality, consistently stated his goal was to save the Union and not end slavery, and allowed slavery to continue in the "border" States of Maryland and Delaware during the War, yet is revered as the "Great Emancipator."

He wanted to let the South "up easy" and spoke of "malice toward none," yet condoned large scale total war operations in the final years of the war and refused to exchange or properly care for tens of thousands of Confederate prisoners of war, even after Union medical professionals pleaded for better supplies.

He spoke of liberty and free government, and yet had over ten thousand Northerners arrested for dissent during the War (many of whom languished in prison for the duration of the conflict), had half of the democratically elected Maryland legislature thrown in jail, unconstitutionally suspended the writ of *habeas corpus*, had partisan hacks in the United States Postal Service search and confiscate mail from political opponents, and supported the illegal placement of troops at polling places and the suppression of free elections.

He is often seen as the embodiment of popular will, yet he received only 39 percent of the total popular vote in 1860 (with over 80 percent voter participation), the second lowest in percentage for a victorious candidate in American history and squeaked by in 1864 even though a Union victory appeared more likely at the time of the election and wide-spread voter fraud boosted his vote total.

He is considered to be the best president in American history, yet the three living former presidents at the time (Buchanan, Pierce, and Fillmore) all characterized his actions during the War as unconstitutional usurpations of power.

"Honest Abe" was a politician. Perhaps nothing more needs to be said.

Mt. Rushmore Myth

TWO MILLION PEOPLE TRAVEL ANNUALLY to South Dakota to see Mount Rushmore. The imposing sculptures of Washington, Jefferson, Teddy Roosevelt, and Abraham Lincoln have become a symbol of the American spirit. The artist in charge of the project, Gutzon Borglum, intended his work to be a summary of the first 150 years of American history, but the choice of figures has helped create a lasting problem in American history: who owns the founding tradition? Borglum has led many Americans to believe that Lincoln and Roosevelt constitute the bridge between the founding generation and the modern era. While there were certainly times Lincoln and Roosevelt could rhetorically *sound* like the Founders, their actions do not mesh with the principles of that generation. Lincoln and Roosevelt helped create a "new" United States, perverted the founding documents and ruined the founding principles of limited government and state sovereignty.

The true expositors of the founding tradition are not the sectional president, Lincoln, or the first progressive president, Roosevelt; they are two Unionists who are often classified as Southern extremists: John C. Calhoun of South Carolina and John Randolph of Roanoke, Virginia. These men were on the cusp of the founding generation. Calhoun was born in 1782 and Randolph in 1773. They were too young to participate in first events of the early republic but knew many of the participants. Most importantly, they understood what the founding generation meant by "union."

The Founders forged a union based on the consent of the States – a compact among them – for their benefit through defense and commerce. They recognized sectional differences and knew that these differences should be respected. Thus, many in this generation, Northerners and Southerners alike, cautiously guarded the interests of their communities through the sovereignty of the states. As long as the benefits and burdens of the union were distributed equally, they suffered and prospered together. Such had been the case in the War for Independence. No one conceived that one section, or one faction should have the right to plunder the other. Madison insisted in *Federalist No. 10* that the Constitution was written to protect against such infractions. Early American documents are littered with statements in defense of a mutually beneficial union. All that ceased in the following two generations.

In an 1833 speech, Calhoun made the following observation:

> "In the same spirit, we are told that the Union must be preserved, without regard to the means. And how is it proposed to preserve the Union? By force! Does any man in his senses believe that this beautiful structure – this harmonious aggregate of States, produced by the join consent of all – can be preserved by force? Its very introduction will be certain destruction of this Federal Union. No, no. You cannot keep the States united in their constitutional and federal bonds by force. Force may, indeed, hold the parts together, but such union would be the bond between master and slave: a union of exaction on one side, and of unqualified obedience on the other."

Such is what Lincoln accomplished through the War Between the States. The South was forced to remain "loyal" under the yoke of the federal government. He preserved the "union," but not the union of the Founders. It was a union of Lincoln's and the Republican Party's creation.

Randolph, in similar fashion, lectured Northern secessionists during the War of 1812 for their stand against the good of the whole. He reminded them that the South had stood shoulder to shoulder with the North during the Revolution and that Virginia had sacrificed far more for the good of the Union by ceding her western lands to the central government than any Northern state in the history of the confederation. Each section suffered due to British hostility, and though Randolph personally opposed the war and foreign alliances, he believed secession during a time of war damaged the prospects of opposition. New England had its chance to secede in 1807 following the Embargo Act, a time of peace, but 1814 was a different story. He said, "Our Constitution is an affair of compromise between the States, and this is the master-key which unlocks all its difficulties."

Randolph was the consistent defender of state sovereignty throughout his career, and he clung to the union of the "good old thirteen states." Likewise, Calhoun insisted that state's rights was the traditional policy of the founding generation. He called Jefferson "the true and faithful expositor of the relation between the States and General Government," and labeled the Virginia and Kentucky Resolutions of 1798 "the rock of our political salvation" in a letter to the citizens of Philadelphia. Only through a firm reliance on state's rights could the government be brought "back...to where it was, when it commenced."

It must be noted that Randolph did not trust Calhoun, and he considered nullification a foolish doctrine (he preferred secession, and did not see how a state could remain in the Union after it nullified a federal law), but when Andrew Jackson as president threatened to use force to coerce South Carolina during the Nullification Controversy of 1832, Randolph said he would strap his "dying body" to his horse "Radical" and enter the field of battle rather than see a sovereign state threatened by the bayonet.

From the 1880 through the 1908 presidential election, there was consistently a clear divide between the North and South. The South voted one way, the North another. Both sections implicitly recognized that the Union was dominated by the North, and no election showcased this more clearly than Roosevelt's victory over Alton Parker in the 1904 election. Roosevelt was not a "national" candidate; he was a sectional one with sectional support. He was not the heir of the Founding Fathers and the founding principles of limited government, state's rights, neutrality, and peaceful trade. He was a bully, an imperialist, and a man who used executive power in a way the founding generation consistently warned against.

Why does this matter? Because Americans are still burdened by factional government and the tyranny of elected despots. We now witness a rural/urban conflict along with a North/South split. Half the population can take from the other half and Americans feel helpless in wake of the political onslaught of "progressivism." But there is hope. Americans still have power in their state and local communities. The states are still sovereign, and Americans have more control over their state and local representatives than those in congress or the executive branch. If Americans recognize that the Union must burden and benefit all equally, as the founding generation, Calhoun, and Randolph emphasized, than there is still hope to salvage the founding principles of the United States. Otherwise, the Founding Fathers will continue to be eliminated from our historical consciousness or will be perverted by progressives such as Barack Obama who invoke their name but know nothing of the founding principles. Mount Rushmore should be split between Jefferson and Roosevelt. That way, Americans could see the canyon – not the bridge – between them.

Solidifying the Cult of Lincoln, Pennywise

IN CASE YOU MISSED IT (I did), Friday was Abraham Lincoln's birthday. In honor of the Great Centralizer, the United States Mint unveiled a new design for the penny. This should put to rest all of the discussion about the elimination of the worthless copper-clad zinc cent, but the real emphasis should be on the new message the penny pushes on the American public: Lincoln "saved the Union" and State's rights is a fallacy. Don't forget it.

The face of the penny will remain unchanged, but the reverse will feature a shield with thirteen stripes and the phrase "E Pluribus Unum" emblazoned across the top. The Mint described the symbolism of the new penny as thus: "The new Lincoln "**Preservation of the Union**" penny is emblematic of President Lincoln's "preservation of the United States of America as a *single and united country*." The 13 vertical stripes of the shield represent *the states joined in one compact union to support the Federal government*, represented by the horizontal bar above [emphasis added]." At the unveiling of the new penny in Springfield, IL, Mint Director Ed Moy said, "This one-cent coin honors the preservation of the union, which was Abraham Lincoln's ultimate achievement. Because of his presidency, despite bitter regional enmity and a horrific civil war, we remained the United States of America." This shield was widely used in the North during the War for Southern Independence as a propaganda piece. Nothing has changed. The penny will be in circulation for at least 50 years.

Senator Dick Durbin of Illinois pushed legislation to redesign the penny through Congress, and it is probably no coincidence that the new penny directly attacks the rejuvenated interest in State's rights and Tenth Amendment issues across the United States. Notice that according to the Mint, the States are in the Union to support the "Federal" government and are a "single united country." That would be news to the founding generation. Outside of the ardent "nationalists" like Alexander Hamilton or James Wilson, very few believed that the States joined in a compact to "support the Federal government." In fact, the Constitution would not have been ratified had this been the case.

Even Lincoln's contemporaries doubted his character and his decision to go to war to "preserve the Union." Few Americans realize that less than forty percent of the American public voted for Lincoln in 1860 and that he narrowly won re-election four years later (he trounced George McClellan in the Electoral College but received only fifty-five percent of the total *Northern* vote. Had the South voted, he would have lost). United States Senator James A. Bayard of Delaware called Lincoln an "ordinary Western man" who had no idea about "republican government." During a three-day speech in 1861, Bayard labeled Lincoln a tyrant and issued this warning:

> You may attempt by war to keep the States united – to restore the Union; but the attempt will be futile. Conciliation and concession may reunite us; war, never! The power may be exercised for the purpose of punishment and vengeance. It may be exercised if you propose to conquer the seceding States and reduce the nation into a consolidated nation; but if your intention be to maintain the Government which your ancestors founded – that is, a common Government over separate, independent communities – war can never effect such an intention.

The other Senator from Delaware, Willard Saulsbury, remarked in 1863 that, "I firmly believe that the usurpation of arbitrary power upon the part of the Executive to arrest peaceful citizens in loyal States has done more to render that disunion of these States, which now is a fact, permanent and eternal, than anything else…." Representative Fernando Wood of New York opined that Lincoln had created permanent sectional animosity by waging war against the South, and more importantly, had destroyed the United States. "Graves in our valleys, sufferers in our hospitals, desolation at every hearthstone, distrust in our rulers, distrust in ourselves, bankruptcy, anarchy, and ruin – these are the triumphs won by your relentless policy."

This is just a scattering of the multitude of comments made in opposition to Lincoln and the War, and to these men, Lincoln did not preserve the United States; he forged a new centralized despotism, the antithesis of the Founders' "united States." The Mint, the Congress, and Americans in general gloss over the fact that many Northerners resisted the Federal draft, believed Lincoln started the War and unnecessarily whipped the North into a bloodthirsty frenzy, and blamed

Lincoln for the destruction of the Constitution. The new penny is another attempt to whitewash the historical record and dupe Americans into believing that Lincoln was the greatest president in American history and the savior of the republic. Those treasonous Southerners deserved the beating they received, and every American, North and South, rejoiced once the Union had been "preserved" and State's rights crushed under the Federal heel. It seems the winds of decentralization have blown into Congress and the propaganda machine is revving up to meet this new challenge to their authority. The misnamed "Preservation of the Union" penny is the clearest example yet. Keep applying the pressure.

Lincolnites are Crazed Warmongers

KEITH OLBERMANN IS AN IDIOT, but you knew that.

He is also a war monger. That was not evident until earlier this month, and Olbermann doubled down yesterday.

Full disclosure. Olbermann once labeled me one of the worst men in America.

Since then, and of course not because of me, his career has gone from bad to worse to in many ways irrelevant, unless you are a blathering idiot on The View or an editor at the *Washington Post*.

On 8 March, Olbermann published an opinion piece in said *Washington Post* declaring he was moving out of one of Trump's New York buildings. Good riddance.

But why is that not funny part? Olbermann objected to Trump's loudmouthed, bombastic public discourse aimed at poking fun of those he doesn't like. This coming from a man who made a name for himself with loudmouthed, bombastic public discourse aimed at poking fun of those he doesn't like. He even admitted his hypocrisy in the piece. But this never stopped anyone on the Left or in the American political class before.

In the midst of this junior high school rant, Olbermann dropped a couple of nuggets that show just how stupid this "brilliant" man is.

Olbermann: "Donald Trump's few forays into actual issues suggest he is startlingly unaware of how the presidency or even ordinary governance works."

I can somewhat forgive Olbermann for this statement. He, like most Americans, has probably never read one sentence from the 1787 or 1788 ratification debates that described how the presidency was supposed to work.

According to *that* Constitution, the president is not a legislator in chief, labor boss in chief, gardener in chief, a scientist in chief, a school principal in chief, or a host of other titles Americans believe the president should hold. In fact, Trump's non-policy policy statements are a refreshing departure from the frivolous boilerplate policy platitudes most presidential candidates spout on the campaign trail. The president was never designed to be anything more than the man who executed the laws of Congress, received foreign diplomats, and led the American military when *Congress declared war*.

That brings me to the most ridiculous statement of the piece.

Olbermann: "And it isn't as though the American electorate hasn't always had a soft spot for exactly the worst possible person for the presidency. Two months before the 1864 vote, some Republicans were so thoroughly convinced that Abraham Lincoln would lose in a landslide that they proposed to hold a second Republican convention and nominate somebody to run in his place. The Democrat they feared, George B. McClellan, was not only probably the worst general in the history of the country, but also, his campaign platform was predicated on stopping the Civil War, giving the South whatever it wanted, running the greatest president in history out of town and repudiating the Emancipation Proclamation. Even after the North's victory at Atlanta turned the tide of the war and thus the election, McClellan — anti-Union, anti-Lincoln, anti-victory and pro-slavery — still got 45 percent of the all-Northern vote."

Not satisfied that only five people read this in the *Washington Post*—I didn't see it until someone alerted me to it—Olbermann reiterated his position on McClellan and the 1864 election yesterday on The View. That might have added a dozen more imbeciles to the list of those who got the scoop firsthand.

This is like throwing Babe Ruth a softball in a beer league game. Olbermann should get that simile.

Lincoln is one of the worst—not the greatest—presidents in American history.

The campaign platform that Olbermann so vehemently disagreed with was actually a *peace* platform designed to stop the bloodletting. To Olbermann, this was bad, for Lincoln's butchering of nearly one million men to "save the Union" was a just war that had to be continued at all cost.

Forget that Lincoln's Emancipation Proclamation was unconstitutional, or that it freed not one slave, or that it would have allowed the Southern States back into the Union *with slavery* if they agreed to stop fighting.

Forget that slavery still existed in the Union until December 1865 and that McClellan said not one word that could be considered "pro-slavery" during the War, other than the same position Lincoln and virtually every other Northerner had at the outset, i.e. slave property was constitutionally protected and would not be confiscated nor interfered with. See the proposed Corwin Amendment that Lincoln supported.

Forget that this "worst general in American" history delivered one of the fatal blows to the Confederate army at Sharpsburg in 1862, a Union victory that allowed Lincoln to issue the Emancipation Proclamation.

Forget that Mr. Lincoln's war was unconstitutional from day one and as per the Constitution the very definition of treason if anyone follows Lincoln's legal logic.

Forget that the Democrat campaign platform explicitly stated, "That the aim and object of the Democratic party is to preserve the Federal Union and the rights of the States unimpaired..." or that the Party sought to restore peace "on the basis of the Federal Union of the States," or that McClellan said after accepting the nomination that, "The preservation of the Union was the avowed object for which the war was commenced." Sounds pro-Union to me.

Of course, the Union the Democrats sought to preserve was not the one Lincoln was remaking. Olbermann's "greatest president in history" was trampling the ballot, suppressing civil liberties, and destroying the Constitution.

The 45 percent of Americans who voted against Lincoln in 1864 were not the idiots. That label goes to the 55 percent who voted for Lincoln, the true "worst possible person for the presidency." A million American graves and the unconstitutional enlargement of executive power are a testament to that fact.

But again, maybe we should forgive Olbermann. Bless his heart. He is, after all, nothing more than an unemployed sportscaster with a big mouth. It should not be expected for such a man to know about anything beyond box scores and jock straps.

That would be like asking a politician to tell the truth, even "Honest Abe."

Republican Tyranny

IN JULY 1862, UNITED STATES SENATOR James A. Bayard wrote to his son before leaving Washington for the summer recess describing the political atmosphere in the United States. "We are living under a petty but ruthless tyranny," he said, "and God knows what folly this admin and its members are not capable of….It is sad, very sad, to think and feel how low the nation has fallen, and how little reason, knowledge of civil liberty, or high tone sentiment or even humanity of feeling is left." He lamented that the American people were "ready for any folly barbarism or brutality those leaders chose to perpetrate." The past year-and-a-half had been a brutal stretch for civil liberty in the United States, and Bayard could sense that things would continue to worsen, particularly in his home State of Delaware. He was correct.

The history of Delaware during the War years is little known, but the actions of the Republican Party in the State expose the ruthless tactics the Party was willing to undertake to root out and destroy political opposition. There is a reason Bayard called the Republicans in Congress and in Delaware "reptiles." They wrecked the election process, violated civil liberties, confiscated mail, and subverted republican institutions for their own partisan gain. The clearest example would be the November 1862 invasion of the State by the United States military with the sole purpose being to influence the elections for both State and federal offices. This event had the consent of both State Republicans, including the candidate for governor and the Republican congressional delegation, and the Lincoln administration, including Abraham Lincoln himself.

Delaware Republicans, namely Congressmen George P. Fisher, feared "Southern sympathy" in the State would lead to defeat in the upcoming elections and thus began to petition the Lincoln administration to take action. Fisher, for whom Lincoln had "a warm feeling and a high regard," wrote the President on 14 August in reference to the November election. Since he had received only a "*plurality*" of 247 votes in 1860, he wanted the Lincoln administration to keep Delaware troops at home to vote in the election. These 500 to 1000 votes, he thought, would strengthen Republican chances of carrying the State. Additionally, Fisher asked Lincoln to postpone drafting troops in Delaware until after the election and urged the administration to strip Democrat Governor William Burton of all appointment powers over the volunteer and militia units of the State. Fisher believed this would save State Republicans from the "fury of our enemies." Lincoln agreed to most of his requests, and stated he was "painfully surprised" to hear of his concern over the matter. He closed his letter by assuring Fisher that he wished for his success "as much as you can wish it yourself." Lincoln's assurances of support would not be enough to placate Fisher and other State Republicans, and by October Delaware Republicans secured Union troops to help influence the election.

The results of the "little" elections in October terrified Delaware Republicans. Democrats swept most local offices in the State, and Republicans feared an impending Democratic victory in the November election. False reports that Southern sympathizers from Maryland would be brought north to help influence the November election, and that hostile Democrats crowded polling places in Kent and Sussex Counties moved quickly through Republican channels. Fisher and Republican gubernatorial candidate William Cannon continued to solicit help from local military officials to put down this Democratic resurgence and help place them in office. In mid-October, between one hundred and one hundred and twenty United States cavalry "paraded" through the State, attended political meetings, cheered for Republican candidates, and insulted the Democratic candidate for Congress, William Temple, and other members of his party, including Bayard. The cavalry remained in the State for two weeks, and most Democrats concluded that the troops arrived to spread alarm and produce "intimidation among the Democrats."

On the Sunday before the general election, Fisher and other Republican officials attended a meeting in Milford, Delaware to discuss the prospects for military occupation on election day. Fisher wanted to petition the federal government for armed intervention in the elections, and the others in attendance agreed that troops were necessary to prevent a Democratic victory. When Fisher's request for troops was initially denied by Secretary of War Edwin Stanton, gubernatorial candidate William Cannon took matters into his own hands by personally asking Colonel James Wallace (a slave-holding Republican partisan) of the Maryland Home Guards to enter the State on election day.

This group had previously been in the State disarming and arresting anti-Republican militia units. Cannon's move was highly irregular, for this request would normally be made by the State Executive, a position Cannon coveted but did not yet occupy. Stanton eventually complied with Fisher's demand, as did Wallace, and days before the election, 1200 troops arrived in Kent and Sussex Counties. The troops were divided into units of between forty and sixty men under the command of Provost Marshals and distributed to polling places throughout the State. The Provost Marshals were considered "active and violent partisans of the Republican party," and were appointed without Governor Burton's authority. In fact, Burton had been given no indication of the impending military invasion by the federal government.

The military presence intimidated voters across Kent and Sussex Counties. Soldiers stood with drawn sabers at the voting window in Georgetown, while Democrats were charged with fixed bayonets in Dover. Some prominent Democrats were required to take an oath of allegiance before voting, and in many cases, Democratic ballots were replaced Republican ballots. Troops arrested and incarcerated Democrats suspected of being disloyal, or those who refused to take the oath, and drove many voters from the polls. Republican officials claimed that troops were necessary to prevent disorder among voters, but when questioned about the subject during a legislative investigation following the election, few Republicans could recall any instances of violence that would have necessitated federal intervention in the State. Troops had been introduced, in the words of one prominent Republican, to prevent being "beaten badly" at the general election.

Unfortunately for the Republicans, the troops did not have the desired effect. Cannon was elected governor, but Fisher lost his seat to William Temple and Democrats gained control of the Delaware Legislature. Following the election, future Delaware Governor Gove Saulsbury formed a committee to investigate the military occupation. After the testimony of over one hundred citizens, most of whom thought "that troops were not necessary on the day of the election, either to preserve peace or ensure a fair election," Saulsbury concluded that the Lincoln administration should be branded "in infamy and everlasting disgrace" for the introduction of troops into "one of the feeblest states in the union, for no other purpose than to determine the result of her local election," for involving the country in a destructive civil war, for suspending the writ of *habeas corpus*, for suppressing free thought and free speech, and for depriving many of life and liberty.

Saulsbury's report is available for free online, but outside of a few State historians, no one knows it exists and it has rarely been cited in academic works. It is a sweeping indictment of the Lincoln administration, particularly in regard to the usurpation of power by the executive branch. If no other event damns the Lincoln administration, the military invasion of Delaware in 1862 should certainly pierce the supposedly impenetrable armor of the Lincoln myth. One can only hope.

(A portion of this essay is reproduced from my dissertation at the University of South Carolina, *A Lonely Opposition: James A. Bayard, Jr. and the American Civil War*)

Apostles of Racism

IF THE MODERN HISTORICAL NARRATIVE is to be believed, then the antebellum North was the happy land of butterflies, flowers, rainbows, and racist free Americans who insisted on racial equality. Only in the South did anyone encounter "Apostles of Racism" as the historian Charles Dew labeled the 1861 Confederate commissioners to other Southern States. But was this so? Would antebellum Southerners have had to convince the majority of antebellum Northerners about their racial positions? Let's see. Printed below are a small sample of the racial positions of several prominent Americans in the 1850s and 1860s.

WHO SAID THE FOLLOWING (answers at the bottom of the quiz)?

1. "As a class the Blacks are indolent, improvident, servile, and licentious."

2. "But the great mass, as they are seen at work, under overseers, in the fields, appear very dull, idiotic, and brute-like; and it requires an effort to appreciate that they are, very much more than the beasts they drive, our brethren—a part of ourselves. They are very ragged, and the women especially, who work in the field with the men, with no apparent distinction in their labor, disgustingly dirty. They seem to move very awkwardly, slowly, and undecidedly, and almost invariably stop their work while the train is passing."

3. "It is not whether we want to associate with the black man...sit by the fireside with them in the social circle, or intermarry with them That is a question of taste."

4. "Down with amalgamation!" or "Separate the Races!"

5. "Missouri for white men and white men for Missouri."

6. "It is certainly the wish of every patriot that all within the limits of our Union should be homogeneous in race and of our own blood."

7. Colonization would "keep our Anglo-Saxon institutions as well as our Anglo-Saxon blood pure and uncontaminated."

8. "I want to have nothing to do with the free negro or the slave negro....We wish to settle the Territories with free white men."

9. Republicans "distinctly and emphatically disavow negro suffrage, negroes holding office, serving on juries and the like."

10. "It is the institution of slavery which is the great parent of amalgamation. Gentlemen need not fear it from those opposed to that institution."

11. "...I will say in addition to this that there is a physical difference between the white and black races which I believe will forever forbid the two races living together on terms of social and political equality."

12. "You and we are different races. We have between us a broader difference than exists between almost any other two races. Whether it is right or wrong I need not discuss, but this physical difference is a great disadvantage to us both, as I think your race suffers very greatly, many of them, by living among us, while ours suffers from your presence. In a word, we suffer on each side. If this is admitted, it affords a reason at least why we should be separated."

13. "And inasmuch as they cannot so live, while they do remain together there must be the position of superior and inferior, and I as much as any

other man am in favor of having the superior position assigned to the white race."

14. "I will say then that I am not, nor ever have been in favor of bringing about in any way the social and political equality of the white and black races."

15. "I have never had the least apprehension that I or my friends would marry negroes if there was no law to keep them from it, but as Judge Douglas and his friends seem to be in great apprehension that they might, if there were no law to keep them from it, I give him the most solemn pledge that I will to the very last stand by the law of this State, which forbids the marrying of white people with negroes."

16. "Our republican system was meant for a homogeneous people. As long as blacks continue to live with the whites they constitute a threat to the national life. Family life may also collapse and the increase of mixed breed bastards may some day challenge the supremacy of the white man."

17. "There is a natural disgust in the minds of nearly all white people to the idea of indiscriminate amalgamation of the white and black races … A separation of the races is the only perfect preventive of amalgamation, but as an immediate separation is impossible, the next best thing is to keep them apart where they are not already together. If white and black people never get together in Kansas, they will never mix blood in Kansas…"

ANSWERS:

1. Abolitionist Horace Greeley of New York, 1855

2. Abolitionist Frederick Law Olmsted of New York, 1856

3. Governor Alexander Randall of Wisconsin, 1859

4. Proposed Republican 1860 campaign slogan by James R. Doolittle of Wisconsin

5. Campaign slogan for Republican Edward Bates, 1860

6. Republican Francis P. Blair of Maryland, 1858

7. Republican James R. Doolittle of Wisconsin, 1858

8. Republican Lyman Trumbull of Illinois, 1858

9. Republican David Davis of Illinois, Lincoln's political advisor, 1858

10. Republican newspaper New York *Tribune*, 1854

11. Republican Abraham Lincoln of Illinois, 1858

12. Republican Abraham Lincoln of Illinois, 1862

13. Republican Abraham Lincoln of Illinois, 1858

14. Republican Abraham Lincoln of Illinois, 1858

15. Republican Abraham Lincoln of Illinois, 1858

16. Republican Rev. James Mitchell of Indiana, 1862

17. Republican Abraham Lincoln of Illinois, 1857

Ready to tear down the Lincoln Memorial? How about the Lyman Trumbull statue at the Illinois statehouse? Maybe the Camp Randall monument in Wisconsin? What about the Horace Greeley statue in New York City? I won't wait around for the protests.

What Would Lincoln Do?

THE REPUBLICANS WON. What's next? In a November 5 opinion piece for the *Washington Times*, Charles Hurt postulates that this could be the "most dangerous two years in 150 years." President Obama, Hurst fears, now has nothing to lose and will become more partisan as he moves farther to the Left. Hurst contends this is a time for statesmanship, for Obama to channel his inner Abraham Lincoln and "save the Republic" as Lincoln did one-hundred fifty years earlier, to look to Lincoln's bust in the Oval Office for inspiration.

Certainly, Hurst has correctly assessed Obama's chosen path. His post-election press conference was little more than a doubling down on the King Barack agenda. Unfortunately, Obama is doing what Lincoln would do. That is what makes him dangerous. Lincoln did not unite anyone except those who insisted on the complete annihilation of the South and the shredding of the Constitution as ratified by the founding generation. Consider Lincoln's actions before the firing on Fort Sumter in April 1861:

> 1. Lincoln privately wrote Republican Senators urging them to reject all compromise measures, including the famous Crittenden Compromise of 1860.

> 2. Lincoln publicly insisted that compromise was not an option in several speeches before his inauguration.

> 3. Lincoln refused to meet with commissioners from several Southern States who were sent to Washington in an effort to settle issues related to federal property and debt. He, in fact, wanted Secretary of State Seward to feign sick to stall negotiations. He did and negotiations never took place.

4. Lincoln ignored the Washington D.C. Peace Conference of January 1861, convened by some of the most respected men in the United States for the express purpose of avoiding war.

5. Lincoln's First Inaugural Address was combative and defiant and placed the burden of compromise on the South, a section which had already left the Union, and not the North, a section which had relentlessly agitated the bonds of Union over the previous eighty years.

6. Lincoln began polling his cabinet the week after taking office about provisioning Fort Sumter. All except his Postmaster General were against the move. Lincoln supported sending a fleet knowing it would lead to war. As he later said to a friend, the action had the desired effect. The South fired first and Lincoln could call for troops by insisting the South started the War.

7. The highest-ranking general officer in the United States, Winfield Scott, argued against any action that might incite violence. He was quickly dispatched from any advisory councils and later made irrelevant by the Lincoln administration.

Remember also that Lincoln was elected with less than forty percent of the total popular vote, was not on the ballot in several States, and did not receive one Electoral College vote south of the Mason-Dixon. He was a minority president with an agenda that sixty percent of the American population rejected in 1860.

Lincoln's partisanship and resolute dedication to the "party line" led to the War in 1861. He refused to compromise, refused to work with those who opposed him, refused to listen to those who wanted to avoid war, and refused to deviate from his agenda. Sound familiar?

Hurst has bought the Lincoln myth of the grand statesman unwillingly dragged into war by hell-bent "fire-eaters" in the South, and who through skilled maneuvering rescued the federal republic of the founding generation and preserved a "government of the people, by the people, and for the people." The story is much more complicated. American collective infatuation with "Honest Abe" is a mental roadblock and destructive to a civil society based on "consent of the governed."

Republicans, for all of their faults, should be ready for a Lincolnian executive, one in which the rule of law is trumped by executive action, separation of power is held in contempt, and the Constitution is nothing but an unenforceable piece of parchment. But to do so, they need to end their love affair with the sixteenth president and recognize President Obama as part of the Lincolnian tradition. That would take a manly determination and a critical reassessment of their core beliefs.

Let's hope the outcome in 2015 isn't the same as in 1861.

A Lonely Opposition

ON 20 MARCH 1861, United States Senator James A. Bayard of Delaware began a three day speech on the prospects of war and the legality of secession. He began by offering a resolution in the hope of avoiding what he predicted would be a long, bloody conflict. It read:

> Resolved by the Senate of the United States, That the President, with the advice and consent of the Senate, has full power and authority to accept the declaration of the seceding States that they constitute hereafter an alien people, and to negotiate and conclude a treaty with "the Confederate States of America" acknowledging their independence as a separate nation; and that humanity and the principle avowed in the Declaration of Independence that the only just hosts of government is "the consent of the governed," alike require that the otherwise inevitable alternative of civil war, with all its evils and devastation, should be thus avoided.

Today, November 15, is Bayard's birthday. His is one of the most important but forgotten United States Senators in American history. There are no monuments to his honor, no buildings named after him, and outside of Delaware hardly anyone has heard his name, but he was one of the few men in the Congress with the resolve to resist the headlong rush to war the Lincoln administration and the Republican Party foisted on the American people, North and South. He privately called Lincoln an "ordinary Western man" that had no concept about American government. Bayard was a rock, a crusader waging what seemed to be, at times, a one-man defense of the Constitution and the Union of the Founders. He was threatened by mob violence, his mail was searched and was later confiscated, he was denounced in the press as a traitor, was hung in effigy in Philadelphia, and later resigned from the Senate rather than continue among the "reptiles" in Congress as he called them. Such a man deserves our attention.

Bayard openly questioned the motivation behind the war against the South and wondered aloud how people could defend such a cause. "Could there be a more revolting proposition than that the individual man, who is domiciled in the State, and residing there, shall be held in the position that he is guilty of treason against the State if he does not side with her, and of treason against the General Government if he does?" He contended "humanity alone" must side with the "law of domicile" in such a situation. When his son-in-law joined the Union army in 1861, Bayard warned, "In embarking on this war therefore, you enlist in a war for invasion of another people. If successful it will devastate if not exterminate the Southern people and this is miscalled Union. If unsuccessful then peaceful separation must be the result after myriads of lives have been sacrificed, thousands of homes made desolate, and property depreciated to an incalculable extent. Why in the name of humanity can we not let those States go?"

In a July 1861 speech entitled "Executive Usurpation," Bayard roasted the Lincoln administration and lamented the loss of liberty. The Constitution "which we had supposed gave us, as citizens of a free country, free institutions, in contradiction to the absolutism which reigned in France" was being subverted by an administration that smacked of Louis XIV, Oliver Cromwell, or Napoleon Bonaparte. Personal liberty was the cost of centralization. "If [you cherish] the principle of civil liberty, [you] cannot sustain this action of the President [suspension of *habeas corpus*] which violates the laws of the land, and abolishes all security for personal liberty to every citizen throughout…the loyal States….power always tends to corruption, and especially when concentrated in a single person."

Bayard typically reserved his harshest statements for the Republican leaders in Congress. He wrote in late 1861 that, "Their intent is the devastation and obliteration of the Southern people as the means of retaining power, and yet I doubt in the history of the world has ever, with the exception of the French reign of terror, shown so imbecile, so corrupt, so vindictive rulers over any people as those with which this country is now cursed." He voted against appropriating money for the war effort, was dismayed by the reckless government spending – "God help the tax-payers if the money can be borrowed" – urged his son to buy gold when the National Bank Acts passed, thundered against their attempts to expel members of Congress for their opposition to the War, denounced troops at the polls, the military occupation of Delaware, and the arrest of dozens of

Delawareans for suspected disloyalty, and believed that the "more moderate" Republicans were being "governed by the violent and ignorant." He wrote, "If the people of the U.S. were not more practical and informed than the element the French Jacobins dealt with I believe we should have the atrocities of the 'Mountain' renewed. Fear alone sustains them." In 1862 he wrote, "State necessity has always been pleaded for the suppression of liberty."

Recent events, of course, make Bayard relevant. Tomorrow, thousands of Americans will flock to see Stephen Spielberg's new film about "Honest Abe," and will doubtless leave feeling a surge in admiration for the "Great Emancipator." Assuredly, Bayard's description of events will not make the film. At the same time all fifty States and over 675,000 people and counting have petitioned the White House to accept the peaceful separation of their State from the Union. Barack Obama has compared his administration to Lincoln's. Perhaps the two have more in common than he realizes.

Lincoln, the dishonest, Hamiltonian, dictator, and Obama, the Marxist, Keynesian, emperor, both have shredded the Constitution, and both have faced a decision on how to handle open defiance of their administration. Obama's will mirror Lincoln's, at least in regard to the legality of secession. Secession, he will say, is illegal, unconstitutional, treasonous, and unpatriotic. And why not, he has so-called conservative support. Bayard said in 1861 that "I believe the great value of the American Union…is the preservation of liberty – by which I mean a Government of laws, securing the right of free speech, securing the freedom of thought, and securing the free and ample discussion of any question." The American people may not be ready for secession and are going about it the wrong way, but let's hope there is a James Bayard in the current crop of United States Senators, someone with the manly resolve to contest the flimsy arguments that will certainly be used against the American principles of independence and self-determination. I don't have much optimism.

The Five Most Underrated Presidents

THE RISE OF RON PAUL in the Republican primary season has raised questions about what Americans expect from the executive office. The accepted interpretation of presidential powers and executive effectiveness centers on the "use" of the office. "Active" executives, such as Abraham Lincoln, Franklin Roosevelt, Teddy Roosevelt and Woodrow Wilson, are usually considered "great," while those who did "little" in office round out the list. For example, a 2010 Siena Research Institute survey included both Roosevelts and Lincoln in the top five while Wilson, Dwight Eisenhower and Harry Truman were in the top ten. The bottom dwellers included Andrew Johnson, John Tyler, James Buchanan and Franklin Pierce. Grover Cleveland and Martin Van Buren were also in the bottom half.

Even lists of great "conservative" presidents like the one produced for Human Events last year include Lincoln, a man who was never considered "conservative" in his time, Dwight Eisenhower, the intellectual progenitor of "compassionate conservatism" (he called it "dynamic conservatism"), and Harry Truman, the man who nationalized portions of the American economy and built his 1948 re-election campaign around *an attack on conservatism*! Each should not be anywhere near such a list. The mark of a great conservative president should be his adherence to the Constitution. "Constitutional" and "conservative" are synonymous, and if exceptions are made, then all the table-thumping about the Constitution falls flat on its face. Exceptions cannot be made. Either American conservatives want constitutional government, or they do not. Any acceptance of a "gray area" leads to further arrogation of power in the executive branch and the destruction of the Constitution *as ratified* by the founding generation. With that said, here are the top five most underrated presidents as defined by their devotion to their oath to uphold and defend the Constitution of the United States:

Part II: Lincolnites, Neoconservatives, and Progressives

1. John Tyler: Short of George Washington, Tyler is perhaps the greatest president in American history. Tyler used his veto power the way Washington intended, as a check on unconstitutional legislation. He vetoed the re-incorporation of a central banking system, as well as bills involving internal improvements and a protective tariff. The Whigs expelled him from the party for "gasp!" following the Constitution. His administration laid the groundwork for the settlement of the Oregon dispute with Great Britain and brought Texas into the Union.

2. Grover Cleveland: Cleveland is well regarded in conservative circles, but he is still generally underrated. Cleveland issued more vetoes than any other president until FDR, and he did so to thwart unconstitutional legislation. He favored low taxes, light spending, low debt and low tariffs. He was the last traditional American conservative in the executive office, and he railed against the growing push for American imperialism.

3. Martin Van Buren: Van Buren advocated low taxes, low debt and low tariffs as president and pushed for a sound money policy. His "independent treasury" eventually rescued the American economy from inflation and a deep depression. He sought to continue the founding tradition by making the United States a peaceful trading partner with the rest of the world. Peace at home and abroad was his primary goal.

4. James Monroe: Monroe was the last of the founding generation in the executive office but is generally ignored by the American academy. Like the other men on this list, Monroe used his veto the way Washington intended. He vetoed an internal improvements bill because he could not find any authority in the Constitution for Congress to pass such legislation. The "Monroe Doctrine" of 1823 codified the American tradition of non-intervention.

5. James Buchanan: This one may shock everyone reading this article. Buchanan is typically in the bottom two of any presidential ranking. But, in contrast to the man who succeeded him, Buchanan worked to avoid war. It must be remembered that there were still eight slave states in the Union in March 1861 when Lincoln took office. Buchanan, in his refusal to attempt to coerce the seven seceded states of the Deep South, forestalled war in the hope of peace. Even Lincoln's own advisers — most importantly Secretary of State William H. Seward and his top general Winfield Scott — attempted to persuade Honest Abe in 1861 that war could be avoided. He refused to listen, whereas Buchanan did. Buchanan should be commended not scorned for such action. He also favored light taxes, low, revenue-only tariffs and the Union of the Founders, meaning one section or group of states (in our day an urban/rural or taxpayer/non-taxpayer split) should not be allowed to abuse the others. How refreshing.

The Five Most Overrated Presidents

ABOUT A YEAR AGO I wrote a piece for The Daily Caller entitled "The Five Most Underrated Presidents" in which I argued that John Tyler is the best president in American history. With the election over, I thought I'd revisit this idea by writing a piece about the most overrated American executives. Most of these men are near the top — typically in the top five — of "historical" American presidential rankings. So, they have to be great, right? Wrong.

Most of the polls are biased in favor of American presidents who personify the active, "bully-pulpit" blueprint Americans seem to think the Constitution established. That is the problem. With the exception of Washington (and even he had an episode or two where his actions were questionable constitutionally) and Jefferson, most of the men at the top of these rankings blatantly and knowingly violated the Constitution during their presidencies. Is that what Americans want? Do we want elected kings with limitless power? With that in mind, here are the top five most overrated presidents in American history:

1. Abraham Lincoln: Lincoln is typically regarded as the most important man in American history and his aggregate score places him higher than George Washington in virtually all "historical rankings." With the Steven Spielberg film ready to hit theaters this week and with Barack Obama (see number five) openly claiming that he is the next Lincoln, perhaps it would be better for Americans to understand the real Abraham Lincoln.

Lincoln was called a dictator and a tyrant by many Northerners for his blatant abuse of the Constitution. Among his detractors were former president Franklin Pierce, famous American authors Nathaniel Hawthorne and Herman Melville, Supreme Court Chief Justice Roger Taney, abolitionist Lysander Spooner and a host of newspapermen and congressmen who viewed his unconstitutional acts — suspending *habeas corpus*, blockading Southern ports, sending soldiers into battle without a declaration of war — with disdain. And, as African-American historian Lerone Bennett, Jr. has shown, Lincoln was hardly the savior of black America.

2. Franklin D. Roosevelt: Almost always listed as the first, second or third greatest American president, "King Roosevelt" is the antithesis of the ideal American executive, and if the founding generation thought someone like Roosevelt would occupy the executive office, the Constitution never would have been ratified. Perhaps only Alexander Hamilton would have wanted a president to have as much power as Roosevelt, but even Hamilton might have objected to such a powerful executive. As I point out in my new book, *The Politically Incorrect Guide to Real American Heroes*, Roosevelt should be castigated for his flagrant abuse of the Constitution, from the obviously unconstitutional New Deal and his so-called "bank holiday" to the creation of "dictators" — we call them czars — and the establishment of concentration camps during World War II. By 1945, 25 percent of Americans depended on the government for some form of income. Thanks, FDR.

3. Woodrow Wilson: Wilson was the model progressive president and is typically regarded as a top-five or at minimum top-ten American president. He is vastly overrated. Wilson hated the United States Constitution, thought that the president needed to be more influential in American politics, created the notion that the president should act like a prime minister by initiating legislation (unconstitutionally) and dragged the United States into World War I to "make the world safe for democracy." Just 20 years later, the United States was involved in a larger and more destructive and bloody war. How did that work out? He nationalized the economy during World War I, advocated the establishment of the Federal Reserve, had over 100,000 people arrested for "sedition" (speaking out against the war) and generally trampled American liberty. The war paved the way for dictatorial powers, and FDR emulated Wilson's domestic programs during World War II. It is no coincidence that two of the bloodiest military conflicts in American history took place under progressive presidents. That alone should place them near the bottom of historical rankings.

4. Teddy Roosevelt: Uncle Teddy was the first progressive president and the first to believe the executive branch was the "bully pulpit." His Square Deal was the model progressive legislative program and gave subsequent presidents the idea that they needed a legislative agenda — Wilson's New Freedom, FDR's New Deal, Truman's Fair Deal, Eisenhower's Dynamic Conservatism, Kennedy's New Frontier, Johnson's Great Society, etc. Teddy took guidance from the intellectual father of modern liberalism, Herbert Croly. Croly argued for an imperialist foreign policy (TR delivered), the fusion of government and corporate America (TR delivered) and a more active central government (TR delivered). In fact, Teddy Roosevelt paved the way for the more powerful presidents who followed.

5 (tie). Lyndon Johnson and Barack Obama: Obama has already been placed in the top tier of historical rankings and he still has one term to go. Americans have been swept up in Obama-mania and because of the historic nature of the 2008 election (which said more about the American electorate than Obama himself), the 44th president is bound for a permanent place in the American pantheon of "great presidents." He doesn't deserve it. From trillion-dollar deficits to continually high unemployment to presidential kill lists and a non-ending war in the Middle East, not to mention Obamacare and the erosion of our civil liberties, Obama should rank in the bottom five, not the top tier. He is every bold progressive president on steroids and HGH.

Johnson wasn't much better. The Great Society and the expensive war in Vietnam forced the country to abandon the gold standard and led to the inflation of the 1970s. We are almost there again. His "war on poverty" was an abject failure (poverty is at the same level today as it was in 1964), his bully "treatment" in American politics made Americans believe that the president should be a partisan political knee-capper rather than a leader and his demonization (the infamous Daisy ad) of Barry Goldwater in the 1964 presidential election bordered on insanity. The American people rejected Johnson's policies outright in 1968. If only we could get that lucky again. Still, his Great Society ideals have never vanished, much to the detriment of the Constitution, individual liberty and American principles.

Establishment Historians' Presidents

C-SPAN RELEASED ANOTHER presidential ranking over the weekend, their first since 2009, and predictably many of the worst abusers of executive power found their name at the top of the list—Lincoln, FDR, TR, Truman, LBJ, Obama, Wilson—while those that expressed some fealty to the Constitution are typically buried in the bottom half.

Some of this was undoubtedly due to the methodology. The 122 historians surveyed were asked to rank the presidents based on the following criteria: "Public Persuasion," "Crisis Leadership," "Economic Management," "Moral Authority," "International Relations," "Administrative Skills," "Relations with Congress," "Vision/Setting An Agenda," "Pursued Equal Justice for All," and "Performance Within the Context of His Times."

Absent was the most important: "Upheld his oath of office." That pesky little think called the Constitution always gets in the way, particularly for the modern president.

None of the criteria C-SPAN chose are found in the document. Last time I checked, Social Justice Warrior in Chief was not in the job description, neither was Legislator in Chief, though that is what we have come to expect.

And what does "Performance Within the Context of His Times" mean, anyway? I find it hard to believe that many of these historians rated Andrew Johnson, Franklin Pierce, or John Tyler near the bottom based on anything but presentism. All held views on race that modern Americans consider appalling but were the widely held opinions of the time, and all three used the executive branch to strike down unconstitutional legislation and had the support a large swath of the American population. Johnson and Pierce are often derided for being *too*

Party driven. Last time I inspected the historical record, the Democratic Party they supported was still a major Party during their administrations. It held the majority of seats in Congress while Pierce was in office, and Pierce crushed his opponent in 1852 by nearly 200 Electoral College votes. His successor, James Buchanan, not coincidentally last on the list, won by 60 in 1856 and carried 19 of 31 states. Pierce carried 27 of 31 states. That is a landslide. Modern progressives may find their actions disturbing (that should be a ringing endorsement), but it sounds like both men fit the "context of his times." They won. Obama rubbed that fact in the face of Republicans during his State of the Union Address, and he received thunderous applause. Piece and Buchanan get the bottom of the barrel.

Does Lincoln get a pass on his belief that whites and blacks could never be equal? Or how about Wilson who advocated and then achieved de jure segregation of the federal government? What about TR who believed in eugenics and called Africans "ape-like naked savages," or his cousin FDR who signed an executive order placing thousands of Japanese-Americans in internment camps? Seems they do, because each one of these men is found in the top 11 with Lincoln, FDR, and TR in the top five.

The other problem has to do with the fact that most of the historians surveyed (not all; there are a few good people on the list) are progressives who believe in the power, activity, and authority of the general government, the Constitution be damned. How else could someone like FDR or LBJ make the top quarter while Grover Cleveland and Martin Van Buren—both constitutional stalwarts—languish in executive purgatory? Cleveland issued the most vetoes in American history before FDR, but unlike FDR, Cleveland issued his mainly because the bills in question violated the Constitution. FDR vetoed the legislation because it did not fit his agenda.

Most historians are creatures of habit. Lincoln is considered great because these other historians considered him great. Pierce is bad because these other historians considered him to be bad. The same can be said for most of the other presidents, from top to bottom. Many historians like to think they are "speaking truth to power" when in fact they could not become "establishment," tenured, or prize-winning authors without trumpeting the fashionable and accepted historical trends. The modern historical profession is often groupthink at its worst.

This is precisely why I wrote *9 Presidents Who Screwed Up America and Four Who Tried to Save Her*. My list looks dramatically different. I wrote about Lincoln, FDR, TR, Truman, and LBJ, but not in the glowing terms the C-SPAN survey believes they deserve. All five screwed up America, meaning they continually and willfully violated their oath of office.

And then there is Obama. How his disaster of an administration placed him at twelve is one of the great mysteries of the survey. If "Pursued Equal Justice for All" was weighed as heavily for others as it was for Obama, then Wilson and TR should be dead last. Obama had a vision, but that was it. He could not work with Congress, had no moral authority, lacked administrative and diplomatic skills, and presided over one of the worst economies in American history for the duration of his two terms. Obama destroyed the Democrat Party and set the stage for the modern "woke" social justice movement.

Three of the "Four Who Tried to Save Her" in my book are considered middle of the pack at best by "establishment historians": Cleveland, Coolidge, and Tyler.

Tyler was the greatest president in American history according to the oath of office. The "establishment" doesn't agree, but then again, they don't really understand the original Constitution.

Opponents of the Constitution in 1788 considered the executive branch to be a major defect of the document. Looking at the establishment historians' list, we can see why.

King Barack

IN JANUARY 1788, Luther Martin of Maryland wrote, "And it was further argued, even if he [the President] was allowed a negative, it ought not to be of so great extent as that given by the system, since his single voice is to countervail the whole of either branch, and any number less than two-thirds of the other... ."

Luther was speaking of the debate over the presidential veto at the Philadelphia Convention of 1787. Fear of executive power saturated the debates at both the Philadelphia Convention and the various state ratifying conventions held to give the Constitution its "vitality," as James Madison later wrote. No one in that generation (publicly) wanted an elected king.

Luther consistently railed against it, and it may be surprising to most Americans in the modern age that the president was never intended to be the chief legislator. It would be news to Bloomberg, some liberal bloggers, and even President Barack Obama himself, given his refusal to negotiate with his "bomb-throwing" opponents in this fabricated budget "crisis." According to the Constitution as ratified by the founding generation, this isn't his job. Nor would members of the founding generation agree with the use of the veto as a legislative hammer.

James Wilson of Pennsylvania proposed at the Philadelphia Convention that the president have "an absolute negative" over proposed legislation. He was alone in this fight. Elbridge Gerry of Massachusetts thought this was unnecessary because "the best men in the community would be comprised in the two branches" of Congress. Benjamin Franklin, in one of his rare speeches at the convention, thought that such a power would reduce the legislature into "compleat [sic] subjection to the will of the Executive." And Gunning Bedford of Delaware said that, "The Representatives of the People (the House of Representatives) were the best judges of what was for their interest, and ought to be under no external controul [sic] whatever." George Mason of Virginia was more direct. Such a power, he said, would lead to a dangerous place, an "elective" monarchy.

The fight continued in the state ratifying conventions and in the press. William Findley of Pennsylvania, speaking at the state ratifying convention, argued that the veto power as written dangerously blended the legislative and executive branch because no law could be passed without the president's "revision." "The Impartial Examiner" of Virginia wrote in 1788 that the veto power would be one step toward an absolute monarchy. "If the system proposed had been calculated to extend his authority a little farther, he would preponderate against all — he alone would possess the sovereignty of America."

By that time, of course, the current language of the veto power had already been codified. The president can veto legislation, but a two-thirds majority of both houses could override his veto. Madison thought this would have the same effect as an absolute negative, but he argued the president would never "have firmness eno' to resist the Legislature unless backed by a certain part of the body itself." James Wilson insisted at the Pennsylvania Ratifying Convention that "no bill passes in consequence of having his [the president's] assent…" and that the president would be guided by the "strict propriety of language" in the Constitution, meaning he was not the chief legislator nor could he "read between the lines."

Herein lies the modern problem. Obama's intransigence has the support from Senate Democrats, but it should be Harry Reid and Dick Durbin, not Obama, negotiating with House Republicans. Obama is violating his oath as president in this process. His job is to execute the laws congress passes. He has violated his oath in this regard several times, even as it pertains to Obamacare specifically, and by refusing to "negotiate" with Republicans over a spending bill is unconstitutionally interjecting himself in the legislative process.

The founding generation would agree. The first five presidents — all from the founding generation — issued a total of 10 vetoes in thirty-six years, eight of which were traditional vetoes with a message to Congress explaining their action. All bills were vetoed on constitutional grounds, meaning the president thought the law in question violated the Constitution. Obama cannot say that about the current proposals from the House of Representatives. The Congress is acting within its constitutional power to defund a federal program, one that is constitutionally dubious from the beginning. By grandstanding against congressional power of the purse, Obama has exceeded his authority and has become what the founding generation feared, an elected king.

Unfortunately, he is not alone. Virtually every president in the last one-hundred years has departed from the original understanding of the veto power. Americans on both sides of the political spectrum need to be consistent in their outrage at executive dictatorship. Otherwise, we are left with ever-expanding executive power. Franklin opined in the Philadelphia Convention that, "The executive will be always increasing here, as elsewhere, till it ends in a monarchy." Perhaps he was more right than he knew. The American people are behind arresting this abuse and that disaster that is Obamacare. Congress is right to act.

Obama and the Prize

THE SELECTION OF BARACK OBAMA for the 2009 Nobel Peace Prize should not be a shock, nor should it concern conservative Americans. Since the news hit yesterday, there have been countless references to a Ronald Reagan snub and outright dismay and indignation that someone who helped "end the Cold War" has yet to be recognized while an international newbie like Obama has been awarded the "highest" honor of peace. News flash: the Nobel Peace Prize has always been an award bestowed upon progressive globalists. Progressives have the home field advantage, and the award is often a farce and a rigged selection. A brief analysis of past winners should alleviate the outrage radiating from conservative circles.

Eight Nobel Peace Prize laureates have been members of the Inter-Parliamentary Union, a leading progressive globalist organization that predated the United Nations and has as a prime directive the promotion of world democracy and human rights. That sounds nice, but the United States is not a member, and several member states violate the core principles of the organization. But, one world government, what George H. W. Bush called the New World Order, has been a primary aim of the progressive movement for generations. Several other laureates have worked with The Hague Tribunal, the progenitor of the International Court of Justice and "legal" arm of the globalist movement, and many American proponents of the ICJ believe the United States Constitution should be superseded by international law and ICJ decisions. Progressives rejoice.

The first American to receive the award, Teddy Roosevelt, was better known for his belligerent attitude toward Latin American through the Roosevelt Corollary to the Monroe Doctrine than for his actions for peace. In fact, Roosevelt was a firm proponent of the Spanish-American War and the quest to detach the Philippines and Cuba from Spain. The Republican Party claimed the war was for "humanity's sake," but the resulting Filipino-American War and the general rebuke of American involvement in Cuba should have been a clue that most Cubans and Filipinos did not want to be under the yoke of the United States.

Woodrow Wilson, the next sitting American president to be awarded the prize, publicly pledged to keep the United States out of World War I, but privately maneuvered into a position where war was the only option. His first Secretary of State, William Jennings Bryan, resigned after he concluded Wilson was being disingenuous about his desire to keep the United States out of the war in Europe. Wilson claimed American entrance into the conflict was to make the world "safe for democracy," though his punitive and dictated peace helped spawn World War II twenty years later. Wilson was ultimately given the award for his proposed League of Nations; however, many Americans rightly rejected the League because they believed it would continually involve the United States in wars against "aggression." Wilson's pursuit of "peace" was hardly peaceful.

And the list of American progressive globalists does not end there. Elihu Root, Charles Dawes (author of the retaliatory Dawes Reparation Plan following World War I), Frank Kellogg, Jane Addams, Nicholas Murray Butler (who admired Benito Mussolini), Cordell Hall (the "Father of the United Nations"), Emily Greene Balch, Ralph Bunche (friend of accused communist spy Alger Hiss), George Marshall (who potentially allowed for the rise of communist China), Jimmy Carter, Al Gore, and now Barack Obama fit the bill. This is not to denigrate all of their particular accomplishments, but simply to make a point. If the American nominee is not a leftist, he or she has a minimal chance of winning the award or of even being nominated.

Focusing on Obama's lack of accomplishments misses the big picture. In essence, who cares? Progressive globalists have their man in office, and they are not going to let that go to waste. Even those who support him have admitted the award was politically motivated. American conservatives should show indifference over the award, not because international peace is not a worthwhile goal, but because the progressive methods of achieving it has long involved the subjugation of American sovereignty to a world government or world court, and both organizations are typically headed by democratic socialists. Conservatives have no chance of winning. The best thing to do would be to mock the award, continue the fight against progressive globalism, and say thanks but no thanks to "world peace" that involves a New World Order based on socialism. Of course, Americans have to repudiate that at home first.

Vote Obama! The Robert W. Whitaker Effect

LADIES AND GENTLEMEN, the unthinkable is happening in the United States, and I would like to thank everyone who voted *for* Barack Obama and his Leftist congressional colleagues in the 2008 election cycle. The popular outrage against Bill Clinton in 1994 paled in comparison to the round of spirited debate that has been generated by the "progressive" proposals currently circulating in Washington D.C. From cap-and-trade, to "stimulus" packages, to healthcare "reform," the Left has tipped its hand, believing it has a mandate from the American people to quickly ram the last vestiges of socialism down its throat. Obama may have been disingenuous on the campaign trail – with the exception of a few "gaffs" such as the Joe the Plumber remark – but he has exposed himself since taking office, and we owe it all to John McCain and Sarah Palin.

The McCain/Palin ticket differed little from the Obama/Biden in form, and only minimally in substance. Palin was certainly a wildcard and, in some ways, an anti-establishment addition to a statist ticket. Heck, her husband at one time possibly supported Alaskan independence. But without question, if McCain had won, the United States would have continued on its slow plodding course toward national socialism, though many conservative Americans would have felt secure because the man who held office had an "R" behind his name. See George W. Bush. Americans may be shocked by our current headfirst plunge into third-world communism, but it has spurred the American conservative spirit, a process that has only been possible because Obama won in 2008. This is why conservative Americans should embrace the Robert W. Whitaker voting strategy in future elections.

Whitaker, a populist conservative who spent some time in the Reagan administration, wrote an interesting treatise on American politics in 1976 titled *A Plague on Both Your Houses*. The book attacked the liberal elites of both the Republican and Democrat Parties, but it was his critique of the common policy of "choosing the lesser of two evils" that should have garnered the most attention.

Whitaker wrote: "Today's populist uprising is against both new establishment excesses in the name of social progress and its fake opposition which pushes military-industrial interests in the name of free enterprise and patriotism. We hold to those ideals. It is to professional liberals and professional conservatives who use those ideals that populism says, 'A plague on both your houses!' Beyond the populist reaction lies a new age. Our failures today are due largely to the fact that out policies are geared to fatten the establishments rather than to solve our problems."

He later outlined the limited political "choices" that "populist" Americans had in the Democrats and Republicans. The two had essentially morphed into a statist coalition using populist rhetoric to enhance their own power and economic muscle. Thus, he argued Americans should not choose "the lesser of two evils," but a true third-party candidate or the greater statist or "establishment" candidate of the bunch. That way, things would reach a boiling point more quickly and the de-legitimization of the political process could be corrected by Americans who truly believed in populist ideals. Professional politicians be damned.

Of course, that was 1976, but his statements still ring true in 2009. Americans have been duped to think that "R" or "D" makes a difference, and that if only (insert your favorite Republican or Democrat here) had won, things would be better. The real battle has become statism vs. liberty. Obama is, hopefully, the tipping point. He is the culmination of 100 years of progressive infiltration of the American political system, but Americans need to avoid the trap being set by the major parties, particularly the Republicans.

Returning Republicans to power in Congress in 1995 and to the executive mansion in 2001 resulted in fourteen years of higher debt, greater spending, a housing bubble, suppression of civil liberties, and out-of-control government. We should have expected no less. They are and have been part of the establishment and most are statists. And Leftists have been disappointed in Obama's resistance to their socialist agenda, regardless of how bad the Right has portrayed it. He has pushed the envelope, to be sure, but as the selection of Van Jones as the "Green Czar" illustrated, the Left wants much more. Obama has betrayed Leftists on the war in Afghanistan, the dismissal of Jones, and the elimination of a "public option" from health care "reform." Leftists vote Democrat and continually get left in the cold.

Voters who wish to see "change" should remember this lesson. The only real choices are third-party candidates at the federal level, or if none exists, vote for the person you *don't* want to win or simply don't vote. This will again hasten the de-legitimization of the political process. The forty-five percent of the total voting population who choose not to vote in federal elections are making a solid statement against the federal leviathan. At the same time, Americans should be concentrating their efforts at the state and local level. As I pointed out in Decentralization for Socialists and Why the Tenth Amendment? the state offers the only hedge against cultural, religious, or economic centralization and ultimate annihilation. The states are not perfect but definitely closer to the location of power, and that is precisely what both the Left and Right want: greater control over the direction of the government.

So, in future elections, if a third-party candidate does not suit your political philosophy, vote for the individual who *least* resembles your ideology and then bolster your power by selecting state and local candidates who will push a state rights message. The Right should be privately cheering Obama's election. He is quickly bringing down the Democrat Party. Just don't let the Republicans swoop in and take credit. They need to go, too. Vote Obama and bring down the federal leviathan!

Was the Civil War [sic] Necessary?

TRUMP SUPPOSEDLY stepped in it. Again.

In an interview that aired Monday with Salena Zito, he wondered aloud that if better leadership could have prevented the Civil War [sic].

Trump thought that Andrew Jackson would have prevailed in a showdown between the North and the South. After all, he did it before in the 1830s. Trump then said this: "He [Jackson] was really angry that he saw what was happening with regard to the Civil War, he said, 'There's no reason for this.'"

Trump followed up by committing the most heinous of all heinous acts. He questioned if the Civil War [sic] was necessary!

The leftist media immediately pounced, with several openly mocking Trump for believing that Andrew Jackson was alive in 1861.

A *USA Today* headline read: "Note to Donald Trump: Andrew Jackson wasn't alive for the Civil War."

The *LA Times*: "Trump makes puzzling claim about Andrew Jackson, Civil War." The Chicago *Tribune* ran the same headline (groupthink) as did a number of other "news" outlets.

Social media trolls ran post after post criticizing Trump's "revisionist" history, lambasting him for not knowing when Jackson was alive, or that he dared to buck modern historical interpretation. The snarky liberal establishment dimwit historian Kevin Kruse Tweeted "When the Civil War came, Andrew Jackson had been dead fifteen years."

Zing! You nailed him Dr. Kevin. How bright! How engaging! Only a Princeton prof could have come up with that one.

The congratulatory remarks rolled in from his "esteemed" colleagues.

And then *The Atlantic* staff lowered the boom. At least that is what they thought.

In only a matter of hours, this "news" magazine published two pieces on Trump's supposed gaffe.

Young leftist twit David Graham published a piece titled "Trump's Peculiar Understanding of the Civil War." in which he made a number of "peculiar" claims himself.

Graham suggested that: 1) "nullification" is unconstitutional because the federal courts say so. 2) "The Civil War [sic] was fought over slavery, and the insistence of Southern states that they be allowed to keep it." 3) The Civil War [sic] wasn't tragic because the "great thinker" Ta-Nehisi Coates said so in 2011. 4) War was inevitable because of the "Confederate states' commitment to slavery." 5) If Trump had read great history like Doris Kearns Goodwin's Lincoln biography *Team of Rivals*, he would have a different position on the War—this position is hysterical.

Graham also dusted off the "Dunning school" pejorative in order to show his supposed intellectual superiority to the sitting president. After all, Graham insisted that Trump can't be blamed for being such a dunderhead because even though he attended great schools, "Many Americans are still taught, incorrectly, that the war was essentially a conflict over state's rights, with abolition as a byproduct of the war. This revisionist view flourished after the war, and though gradually being displaced, is common across the country."

This is the revisionist calling traditional history revisionism.

The Atlantic followed up just over an hour later with a piece by Yoni Applebaum titled "Why There Was a Civil War." The revisionist hits just kept coming.

Applebaum didn't berate Trump for *suggesting* that historians don't ask if the Civil War [sic] could have been avoided—he proved that this has been done for years by going through about a century of American historiography on the issue—but for *claiming* that the War could have been avoided and by "the omission of a critical word: slavery." To Applebaum, the question of the War begins and ends with slavery and nothing but slavery. He provided one quote from Lincoln to prove his point and as most shallow Lincoln apologists do today, several quotes from the Southern States' declaration of causes that seem to prove unequivocally that slavery and only slavery led to the War.

He concluded his article with a strange application of moral causation to the War, a moral causation that the vast majority of Americans missed in both 1860 and 1861 when the question of war or peace was still on the table. "There are some conflicts," he wrote, "that a leader cannot suppress, no matter how strong he may be; some deals that should not be struck, no matter how alluring they may seem. This was the great moral truth on which the Republican Party was founded."

If only it were that simple. And if only Lincoln was the great leader that both Graham and Applebaum believe him to be.

It seems both Graham and Applebaum fell asleep in class or at the very least have swallowed the Lincoln myth so thoroughly that no evidence to the contrary could persuade them of their folly or their revisionism.

Certainly, Trump is no scholar and his reverence for Jackson is troubling, for it was Jackson who provided the blueprint for Lincoln's heavy-handed tactics toward the South in 1861. To suggest that he would have worked out a compromise is a stretch, though he did support the deal Henry Clay brokered with South Carolina in 1832, a deal that resulted in the people of South Carolina nullifying the Force Bill and then heading home.

That is often lost in the story. Nullification worked and contrary to what Graham suggested, the federal court system has never had the final say on the constitutionality of nullification. That was always the point. States don't ask permission from the federal courts to nullify unconstitutional legislation, and as every proponent of the Constitution swore in 1787 and 1788, including Alexander Hamilton and James Wilson, laws contrary to the Constitution would be void. Jefferson and Madison made it clear the States could void them.

The real problem with both pieces in *The Atlantic*, however, is the insistence that the War was inevitable and some moral conflict over slavery caused the shooting.

Applebaum understood that the entire fabric of early American history was built on compromise, but Graham seemed to miss that.

Based on the history of the United States, there was never an "irrepressible conflict" until the North decided to fabricate one.

The South, in fact, was willing to compromise in 1860 and 1861, as it had been for the eighty years prior. Jefferson Davis insisted that any compromise placed before the special Committee of 13 established to handle the crisis needed the support of both Republican and Democratic members. He could get the Democrats to support several. But the Republicans, at the insistence of president-elect Lincoln, said no to every single one. Is that the work of a leader?

That led six other Southern States out of the Union in early 1861. Lincoln could still have saved the Union through compromise at this juncture but chose not to do so. As Senator James Bayard of Delaware stated in 1861, the Union still existed even with seven States missing. The government, banking houses, and infrastructure remained. It seems that the "Confederate States insistence on slavery" had nothing to do with War. War and secession are separate issues. Secession didn't mean war was inevitable. Most Americans hoped otherwise, even in the South where President Davis insisted that the South simply wanted to be left alone. To think the opposite is to assume the posture of the British in 1776. That is un-American.

There were still six other slave States in the Union as late as April 1861, over a month after Lincoln took office, six slave States that had already rejected secession. Lincoln was not worried about slavery at this point. He supported a proposed thirteenth amendment which would have protected slavery indefinitely in the States where it already existed. He promised never to interfere with the institution in the South. Lincoln's objective in March 1861 was to "preserve the Union" at all costs, and by "preserving the Union" Lincoln meant preserving the Republican Party and his fledgling administration. Letting the South go would have certainly made him a one term president. He received less than forty percent of the popular vote in 1860.

Applebaum is correct that letting the South go would have ensured the existence of slavery both within the Union and out for the near future (every other power abolished slavery by 1880), but this was not a moral question for most Americans. Lincoln received thunderous applause across the *North* in 1860 when he made promises to leave the institution alone. Racism was an American institution and Lincoln never challenged the prevailing attitudes on blacks. He embraced them. The Republican Party didn't dabble in "moral truths." Their objective was always political. Bottle the South up, ensure that the Whig economic agenda could be ascendant, and control the spoils.

This still doesn't take away from the tragedy of the War. Contrary to what the "great scholar" Coates had to say—and he has as much claim to being a great scholar as David Barton, which isn't much—the loss of one million men, the best blood in America, to a war for Union as Lincoln insisted was unnecessary at best and diabolical at worst. The elimination of slavery was for much of the war an afterthought. Lincoln considered it nothing more than a war measure to "best subdue the enemy."

The simple fact is that Lincoln wanted war. He had the chance to save the Union without war before he took office. He had the chance to save the Union without war in March 1861. He rejected attempts to peacefully purchase federal property and began polling his cabinet about provisioning Sumter less than a week after taking office knowing full well it would cause war. As he later told a political ally, his decision to provision Fort Sumter had the desired outcome, meaning armed conflict. Nothing can sugarcoat Lincoln's headlong rush into the bloodiest war in American history.

Trump may have been on to something here. Better leadership could have avoided the carnage. But saying that is now considered sacrilege. How closed minded of the "liberal" historical profession and establishment gatekeepers of acceptable truth.

But who cares. No one really reads *The Atlantic* anymore, anyway.

The American Tradition is Anti-War

TWO RECENT SEEMINGLY INCONGRUOUS EVENTS present symptoms of a larger disease in the American polity.

First, North Korean dictator Kim Jong-Un has promised to nuke the United States, and according to recent testimony before Congress, a North Korean EMP attack could kill 90% of the American population within one year.

Second, on Monday, October 16, the National Infantry Museum in Columbus, GA dedicated the "Global War on Terrorism" memorial. Highlighted are the over 6,000 American soldiers killed since 2002 in the modern campaign to "make the world safe for...."

The world wasn't too safe for them or apparently for the almost 300,000,000 people who could be wiped out by a reckless Marxist thug with an itchy trigger finger. They are real and potential casualties—symptoms—of a disease that has consumed American life since the early twentieth century: American sabre rattling.

You see, the anthem protests, our worship of the military industrial complex, and making every event from the local civics meeting to an NFL game a setting for "patriotism" has provided the kindling for a massive military bonfire.

All it takes is a little spark. But it hasn't always been so.

The modern neo-cons will tell you that Americans have been warlike from the beginning, that almost unanimous support for World War II was the rule rather than the exception. That is a lie.

There is a long-standing anti-war American tradition.

Probably half, perhaps the majority, of the British North American colonists wanted a peaceful solution to the constitutional crisis that became the American War for Independence. "The Penman of the Revolution" John Dickinson's famous "Olive Branch Petition" was not some shot in the dark. He was a serious man dedicated to exhausting all peaceful avenues to the crisis before taking up arms even after the shots at Lexington and Concord in 1775. He wasn't alone and loyalty to the cause often fluctuated during the hard years of war.

New England had to be dragged kicking and screaming into the War of 1812, an event they labeled "Mr. Madison's War." Americans had justifiable reasons to go to war with Great Britain in 1812, but that did not mean support for the conflict was unanimous.

"Mr. Polk's War" with Mexico in 1846 faced considerable congressional opposition for various reasons. Abolitionists feared it would add new slave territory to the United States and called it part of a "slave power" conspiracy. This attack should have fallen on deaf ears. The recognized "defender of slavery" in Congress, John C. Calhoun, opposed the war because he feared its impact on executive power. He was right. Polk just wanted California and by getting it greatly expanded executive authority.

The War for Southern Independence saw opposition on both sides of the Mason-Dixon though far more pronounced in the North. Lincoln didn't call it the "fire in the rear" because it lacked teeth. Thirty-thousand Northern civilians were arrested during the War for their opposition to the Lincoln regime, newspapers were shut down, and congressmen booted from their seats (or sent packing to Canada). In the South, Davis faced constant sniping about his leadership, war plans, and abuse of power from the opposition press. Even before the War began, various civic and political leaders wondered aloud why the North couldn't just let the States go in peace, among them the abolitionist Lysander Spooner and United States Senator from Delaware James A. Bayard. Davis insisted in his first inaugural address that the South simply wanted to be left alone. Neither Lincoln nor a potential war were that popular during the "secession winter" of 1860-61.

The Spanish-American War of 1898 led to the birth of the American Anti-Imperialist League. This organization was an eclectic collection of political, religious, civic, and social leaders dedicated in their opposition to American expansion overseas. This "splendid little war" also gave William Graham Sumner the idea to pen his splendid essay "The Conquest of the United States by Spain" which laid bare the problems of American global aspirations.

Woodrow Wilson won in very close 1916 presidential election because he "Kept Us Out of War" in Europe. That was never his goal, and he pivoted shortly after winning the election, but the majority of the American public rightly did not want to send its boys to Europe to die in our first global crusade for democracy. That wasn't the only outcome of the war. Massive expansion by the general government followed our charge "Over There" and the modern American bureaucratic nightmare in Washington D.C. was born. Throw in a new Sedition Law and over 200,000 political arrests and the Wilson regime did much to shred the United States Constitution.

Even the "unanimous" War with the Axis Powers in 1941 wasn't so unanimous at the beginning. The American First committee led a considerable effort to keep the United States out of the costliest war in human history. They weren't anti-Semitic or pro-German. They were simply anti-war and pro-American. Much of the neo-con attack on people like Charles Lindbergh is based on half-truths and outright lies. Of course, the economic impact of the war is always misrepresented as a positive. People had cash in their pockets (no gold because FDR confiscated that years before) because they couldn't buy anything. Those who voted for Roosevelt to abolish bread lines now had to wait in line to buy sugar and gasoline. That was at least preferable to a grave in Europe or Asia.

Since this last officially declared war in 1941, a large percentage of Americans have been consistently opposed to American adventurism and foreign wars. Korea, Vietnam, the Cold War, and the Global War on Terror have all met opposition, albeit typically for partisan political reasons.

This doesn't mean Americans should not defend our borders and protect our homes. That is a just war. Most Americans, however, still do not want to engage in a foreign policy that invites war, either. Donald Trump was elected in part because of this message. He seems to have forgotten his earlier positions.

Of course, I can't let Alexander Hamilton off the hook in ushering in this mess. He provided the blueprint for the modern imperial presidency, the same presidency that can now send American troops into combat without congressional authorization.

But real "conservatives" have long warned against war. This is one reason they split with the neo-cons in the post-World War II era. They rallied against it, denounced it, and insisted that it would produce a host of horrors. And they were right.

Not only does it create economic and social dislocation, it allows the general government to expand its powers exponentially. That alone makes it dangerous. It is no coincidence that American liberty has suffered most during periods of war and why the American anti-war tradition should be studied and promoted.

Hamiltonian Nationalism

STEVE BANNON'S SEPTEMBER 10, 2017 *60 Minutes* sparked considerable discussion among both the left and the right. Bannon is always good for that.

After Charlie Rose insisted that immigration built America, Bannon retorted that he was wrong and then seemingly reinforced the idea that "nationalism" has defined American history:

> "You couldn't be more dead wrong. America was built on her citizens. ... Look at the 19th century. What built America's called the American system, from Hamilton to Polk to Henry Clay to Lincoln to the Roosevelts. [It was] a system of protection of our manufacturing, financial system that lends to manufacturers, OK, and the control of our borders. Economic nationalism is what this country was built on. The American system."

The left took this as an insult to unlimited immigration and fired off several shrill pieces attacking Bannon's perceived jingoism and nativism. After all, they argued, Alexander Hamilton was an immigrant.

That isn't the problem. Bannon was *correct* about immigration. The United States is not a "nation of immigrants." Hamilton arrived in the British North American colonies from a British Caribbean colony, which meant he technically moved from one British possession to another. That isn't "immigration" as the left defines it.

Most American leaders in the 18th century were third and fourth generation colonials, born in North America, who considered their native colonies their "country." Hamilton was different but no more or less a British subject than Thomas Jefferson or George Washington.

Certainly, immigrants were used as laborers throughout American history, but to suggest that non-citizen immigrants "built" America, as the left does, is to 1) believe that most non-skilled American workers were immigrants (they weren't) and 2) accept the Marxist narrative of history that labor would build things without capital. Both are fallacies.

But that is not Bannon's fault. That is leftist mythology.

Bannon suffers from a different type of mythology, that of the "nationalist myth" of American history.

According to the "nationalist myth," the founding generation *really* wanted a strong central government to cement American exceptionalism, but those pesky states kept acting up and Americans were forced to fight a war to settle supremacy once and for all. As Bannon suggests, it was nationalism that created everything good in America.

Neither Bannon nor the left are to blame for their misreading of American history. We have all been indoctrinated in some way to defend an American historical fairy tale. Hamilton, Henry Clay, John Marshall, Joseph Story, James Wilson, Abraham Lincoln, and other expositors of the "nationalist myth" were definitively "American" and it's easy to read history backwards, to see the present as an inevitable outcome spawned from the dominant vision of American nationalists.

To quote Bannon's response to Charlie Rose, that is "dead wrong" and Hamilton mythmaking is responsible for all of it.

Americans have been led to believe that Hamilton's economic dream is somehow free market capitalism ordained and established by the founding documents. Hamilton's system later became known as the American System which as Bannon suggests capitulated American business into the twenty-first century.

Except the Hamiltonian or American system was not free market anything. It was corruption and crony capitalism of the highest order. Certainly, some people became filthy stinking rich because of it, but they did so because the general government unconstitutionally began picking winners and losers through higher protective tariffs and federally funded internal improvements like road, canals, and later railroads.

Anyone who thinks American taxpayer support for Elon Musk's Tesla brand is a terrible idea can thank Hamilton's crony capitalist system. The same can be said for virtually every Gilded Age railroad magnate. Government corruption stuffed their pockets.

Hamilton wanted it that way. He once told Thomas Jefferson and John Adams that corruption is what made the British constitution the best in the world. Hamilton then did his best to ensure that corruption found its way across the pond often through artful lying. Only nationalism made that possible. If you love political and economic corruption, Hamilton is your guy and nationalism is your standard.

Hamilton's opponents often knew the score. They railed against the fusion of government and finance capital and feared the effects of nationalism on the American political system. Most forget, or more than likely don't know, that these men, the Jeffersonian Republicans, were in the *majority* for much of the first eighty years of American history. Hamilton's financial system never really got off the ground until the Civil War removed all obstacles to strong central control. His "implied powers" vision of government certainly had supporters, particularly in the federal court system where it was codified in several dubious Supreme Court decisions, but Americans consistently sent "strict construction" majorities to Congress throughout the antebellum period.

Hamilton got his Bank of the United States, but it failed re-charter in 1811. Nationalists foisted a Second Bank of the United States on America in 1816, but it failed re-charter in 1836. Central banking did not see the light again until the 1860s, not coincidentally when most of the opponents of Hamiltonianism were out of the Union. Tariffs were typically for revenue only in the antebellum period. That changed during the War. Federally funded internal improvements did not have substantial legislative backing until Reconstruction. Even the greatest nationalist president in the nineteenth century, Lincoln, received less than forty percent of the popular vote in 1860 and only fifty-five percent of an entirely *Northern* vote in 1864. Nationalism was by no means that popular, and it certainly was not constitutional.

Hamiltonianism never won in antebellum America. It took the bloodiest war in American history to enshrine his vision for the United States while concurrently creating the "nationalist myth."

American history has been turned upside down. Economic nationalism did not build America. Neither did Hamilton or the American system. Federalism and rugged individualism sparked the American age.

Hamilton's opponents are regarded as a footnote, the stinging gadfly on the rump of good government, and are largely forgotten. But they were right from the beginning, and we should heed their warnings.

One thing can be said for American nationalism. It has led to every major war, every bad policy, every bit of government corruption at the federal level, and every political conflict in American history. Americans don't like top-down government unless they control the levers of power. The only solution is to rebuke Hamiltonian nationalism and return to the Jeffersonian vision of federalism and limited central power. There would be fewer wars, less political conflict, and a happier and more prosperous people.

That would take a massive paradigm shift, or maybe just a better understanding of real American history.

Hamilton: Liar

REPUBLICANS UNVEILED THEIR TAX PLAN in September to mixed reviews. That was to be expected. It hasn't gotten any better in recent weeks.

Americans generally want lower taxes. They also want the Republican Party to do *something* they promised while begging for votes.

Let's not ask for too much.

One called on the Rush Limbaugh Show in late September suggested that people read *Federalist* No. 21 to understand why taxes should be lowered. Hamilton, this caller said, showed us the light.

Limbaugh joked that he rapped it. Either way, here is Hamilton entering another modern debate. There is now an app for that, unfortunately.

Hamilton proposed in *Federalist* No. 21 that "indirect" taxes, meaning tariffs, should be used more extensively than direct because direct taxes created substantial problems for an economy. The modern income tax is a direct tax.

Except we shouldn't listen to Hamilton. He didn't mean it. Less than three years after writing *Federalist* No. 21, Hamilton turned around and argued for… drumroll…a lengthy list of direct taxes, ostensibly because the country "needed it," but Hamilton suggested that such taxes would only be used in a time of war. The United States wasn't at war in 1790.

That was Hamilton's "m.o." His duplicity knew no bounds.

Which is why he screwed up America.

John Taylor of Caroline called him a tyrant as did a number of forward-thinking Americans at the time. They could see Hamilton's constitutional machinations wrecking the fragile fabric of Union. His top-down approach to every problem and his penchant for advancing a stronger central authority at the expense of the states were the exact opposite positions he favored while scribbling the *Federalist* essays, and many could see that Hamilton's desire to recreate the corruption of the British constitution would eventually destroy the Union.

It wasn't "state's rights" that ripped apart the Union. It was Hamiltonian nationalism, the belief that the general government can do anything it wants as long as it is "necessary and proper" for the "general welfare" of the American people, the Constitution be damned. That is the real story of America, but every school child is fed the opposite narrative from the time they enter kindergarten as a little mind of mush. Uncle Sam knows how to indoctrinate kids, and we want more Uncle Sam in education. Doesn't make sense.

With Constitution Day a little over a month ago, Americans should reconsider their Hamilton love. They should first avoid downloading the app. After all, Hamilton's Constitution, the Constitution he favored in 1787 when he called for unlimited central power or the Constitution he advanced as Secretary of Treasury with expansive "implied powers" was the opposite of the Constitution he sold to the states as primary author of the *Federalist* essays and in speeches to the New York ratifying convention. And he clearly knew it.

Hamilton, for example, knew his "assumption scheme" where the general government would assume the debts of the several states was expressly rejected by the Philadelphia Convention, but he pushed for it anyway. Same with his favorite project, the Bank of the United States. That idea was shot down so thoroughly that no one in Philadelphia in 1787 thought it would be resurrected once the Constitution was ratified. They were wrong.

Hamilton argued in *Federalist* No. 69 that the American presidency would not resemble a king only to push for executive powers while Secretary of Treasury that George III would have recognized.

Hamilton was a brilliant, narcissistic, psychopath, a man with a real "American story" of "rags to riches," but a man who did more to undermine the original understanding of the Constitution—an understanding he helped craft—than anyone in American history.

Conservative Americans should stop rapping about Hamilton and start railing against him. If they truly believe in a general government of limited powers, of real "grass roots" politics, then Hamilton is not their guy.

There is a reason a leftist political activist like Lin Manuel-Miranda wrote a play about Hamilton. That should give any conservative pause. Miranda didn't hijack Hamilton's legacy. He merely lifted the veil.

But by letting Miranda tell the story, "Who Lives, Who Dies, Who Tells Your Story," Hamilton gains a reputation he doesn't deserve. Hamilton's musical should rather be "Hamilton: The Liar."

PART III:
SOUTHERN COMFORT

Please "Dump Dixie"

MICHAEL TOMASKY AT THE DAILY BEAST believes "It's Time to Dump Dixie." Please do. He also thinks that there may be a point in the future when the South should have its independence. Hallelujah, but we tried that once and were forced to keep company with our "kind" neighbors to the North, those like Tomasky who call the South, "one big nuclear waste site of choleric, and extremely racialized, resentment." Tomasky, by the way admits he was born in West Virginia, yet laments it "was not a Southern state when I was growing up but culturally is one now." You see, according to Tomasky, the South lacks "tolerance, compassion, civic decency, trans-racial community, [and] the crucial secular values on which this country was founded...." Translation: America used to be a great progressive wonderland of democracy and equality, but evil Southerners ruined it! Better to just write off Dixie than try to convert them, for, as we all know, the North is the bastion of all things good and noble, the shining city upon a hill for the world to emulate.

Tomasky suffers from a common syndrome known as Yankee Self-Righteous Delusional Disorder (YSRDD). It can be seen in most major metropolitan areas in the North and heard on many nationally syndicated radio and television programs, particularly those that lean Left. You can also find it in Northern dominated tales of their moral and intellectual superiority. See, for example, any major collection of American literature or art. But are the invectives that drip from Tomasky's pen true? After all, one would think with all the hand-wringing over the problematic South there must be something to the progressive narrative of the region.

Let's start with Tomasky's first claim that the South lacks "tolerance" and "trans-racial" communities. According to a study by professors John Logan and Brian Stults, only *eight* of the top twenty-five most racially segregated cities in the United States are in the South, and that includes Miami and St. Louis, two cities that Tomasky considers Northern and Western. Remove those, and *nineteen* of the most racially segregated cities are found in the North, including Chicago, New York City, Philadelphia, Los Angeles, and Detroit. Progress. Perhaps us racist Southerners should look to emulate our good brothers to the North. Examples of modern, progressive meccas of racial harmony abound north of the Mason-Dixon. Probably as a result of YSRDD Tomasky conveniently forgets that the nastiest and most violent of all the race riots of the twentieth century took place in Northern cities. And he probably doesn't know—or doesn't care to know—that according to the *Christian Science Monitor*, black Americans are moving back to the South in large numbers for "economic and cultural" reasons. So much for the South as a hostile, segregated, cultural wasteland of America.

What about civic decency? I am not sure of Tomasky's definition, but this would generally include good manners, hospitality, and charity. Conde Nast Traveler recently released its annual survey of the friendliest cities in America, and surprise, surprise, four of the five friendliest places are in the South, with number one being Charleston, South Carolina. Conversely, all five of the unfriendliest places in the United States are found in the North, with number one–Newark, New Jersey–ranked as the unfriendliest place in the *world* in 2013. That is a big honor for our Northern "friends." At least they are number one in something.

Southerners also love to open their wallets for those in need. The South is consistently ranked as the number one charitable region in the United States with Alabama and Mississippi closely following Utah as the most charitable States in the Union. I guess Southern Bible thumpers hate people so much they want to give them a helping hand. Tomasky does not want to admit it, but Christians actively follow their calling to charity. Faith matters. By the way, the least charitable region in the U.S. is New England, followed closely by New York and California. But who could donate to charity in those States even if the people had the desire? Progressive politicians and heavy-handed government rob their citizens of over fifty percent of their income. John Taylor of Caroline, an evil white Southern plantation owner, had something to say about that in 1814, "A nation oppressed by taxes, can never be generous, benevolent, or enlightened." Tomasky hasn't gotten the memo.

How about "crucial secular values on which this country was founded"? No one would confuse the South with the rampant non-Christian regions of the North and West Coast, thank God, but the South does have a claim to the "secular values on which this country was founded." It was Thomas Jefferson and James Madison, Southerners by the way, who insisted on religious liberty in both Virginia and the United States at large. The most vociferous opponents of this idea could be found in…you guessed it, New England. During the tense period leading to ratification of the Constitution in 1788, many New Englanders worried that the Constitution did not have a religious test for office and complained the new government was too secular. Three New England States had State established churches at the time. Additionally, Charleston, South Carolina earned the nickname the "Holy City" because of its religious diversity, including a large Jewish population. Baptists and Quakers were beaten and killed in New England in the colonial period. Tolerance.

All of this says nothing of Southern contributions to American culture at large, from music (integrated bands in Alabama during the height of segregation), to food, to literature, to political and military heroes, the South has a monopoly on what most people consider "American." No one sings "Sweet Home Massachusetts." Even the Southerners Tomasky likes, Carter Glass of Virginia for example, were reared by a culture he finds deplorable. Southern "populists" were not progressives like Tomasky. They were Jeffersonians, a tradition which was nourished by a Southern taproot.

Thankfully, though Tomasky is a lost cause, YSRDD is a curable disease. Many Northerners, both on the Left and the Right, have found in the South the cradle of all things good in American history and culture. The place makes the people. Every year, thousands of Northerners move to the South to escape the decaying cities, culture, and people of the North. The same can't be said of Southerners. Who flies north for the winter or chooses to retire in Ohio? And for those who don't like it here, as Lewis Grizzard said, "Delta is ready when you are."

Without the South, however, Tomasky and his fellow YSRDD suffering comrades would have no one to blame for all of their problems. They could just look out back, but that would be too easy. Southerners are their bogeyman, which is why they would never (and could never) let us go.

Clyde N. Wilson

MOST PEOPLE DON'T KNOW, but today (June 11) is Clyde Wilson's birthday.

I had the honor of being Clyde's last doctoral student. I first met Clyde in the Spring of 1997 as a senior in college trying to decide where to attend graduate school. My top choices were South Carolina and Alabama, Clyde Wilson or Forrest McDonald. My advisor as an undergraduate, Bart Talbert, attended Alabama and had given me a sound education on all things McDonald. He was one of McDonald's last students.

I left Salsibury, Maryland on my Spring Break determined to find a home for the next several years. I had spoken to Clyde before I left–actually his answering machine–and let him know when I would be arriving in Columbia. South Carolina was my second choice, but I knew of Clyde and his fantastic work on the South and on the Papers of John C. Calhoun. I would be happy there, too, if fate saw fit to send me there.

Clyde's office was located on the first floor of Gambrell Hall, a grey maze of a building that looked like something Stalin's architects designed during the Five Year Plans. It should have been a warning. Some of the professors in the history department would have been comfortable goose stepping around Red Square.

I found Clyde's office, knocked, and in his distinctive way told me to "come in." He shook my hand, leaned back in his chair, and spoke to me for about thirty seconds before two of his students came sauntering into the room.

"This is Carey Roberts and John Devanny," Clyde said, "and they will be showing you around."

That was the last I saw of Clyde. Roberts and Devanny brought me to a little office, turned on the hot lights, and began interrogating me. Why did I want to attend South Carolina? Why did I want to work with Clyde? What did I want to study? And Devanny threw the Oxford dictionary at me. It was akin to reading an Augusta Jane Evans Wilson novel.

I assume I made it through their interview in fine order because Clyde had no objection to working with me. But I still had to meet McDonald at Alabama.

I remember crossing into Alabama with Skynyrd's "Sweet Home Alabama" playing in the background. I still thought Alabama would be my home.

Gary Mills met me at his office in Tuscaloosa, and we went to a local restaurant to chat. Mills was a mountain of a man, as wide as he was tall. I picked a booth and he barely squeezed in. Mills used to go to his office to smoke. His wife didn't like it. He had a large First National behind his desk and spoke so softly that you had to lean in to hear him. He was an honest historian who wrote about Creoles in Louisiana during and after the War, and he loved the South.

He arranged my meeting with McDonald and McDonald's wife, Ellen Shapiro McDonald. It was more like a meeting with Mrs. McDonald. Mills introduced me to the McDonalds and they both politely asked me into Forrest's office. I explained what I wanted to study and how Bart had spoken highly of them. They liked Bart. But Mrs. McDonald very bluntly said, "Go work with Clyde." Perhaps it was because of what I wanted to do, or maybe it was because they didn't want to work with me; either way, my course was set. South Carolina it was.

I thought South Carolina and graduate school would be different. Every one of Clyde's students has a similar story. It was like serving several years in academic purgatory. We were ostracized, criticized, and at times demoralized. The department had it out for Clyde and in turn had it out for us. At least we thought so. There was no conclusive proof, but life in the department was not easy. We were all pariahs, independent thinking students who did not adhere to the "fashionable" trends. Some–the handful of good people in the department both students and faculty–saw that as a benefit; others wanted to marginalize us. Clyde once said that when he arrived at South Carolina he hoped for rigorous academic discussions, real scholarship. He didn't find it, and all of his students soon realized that no matter what we wrote or researched, it would be ignored by the mainstream historical profession.

I was born in Virginia and have spent almost all of my life in Southern States, but my family is not from the South. My perception of the South had been forged as an undergraduate, and I was drawn to the political and philosophical underpinnings of the Southern tradition. But like many Americans, Southerners included, I considered the "South" to be the four-year period between 1861-1865. I had a rather narrow view of Southern history. Clyde changed that.

He once called Jeff Rogers and me to his office to emphasize what we needed to know in order to obtain a Ph.D in history.

He welcomed us in, leaned back in his chair, stroked his beard, crossed his hands on his stomach and said,

"Tell me everything you know about George Washington."

Jeff and I mumbled a few sputtering words about his political and military career.

"No, what about his family life? His childhood? You need to be able to write a several page paper about Washington with no assistance."

Silence.

"Ok, tell me everything you know about Thomas Jefferson."

Again, the same reaction.

"You two have work to do."

Notice Clyde did not ask us about Robert E. Lee or Jefferson Davis. Certainly, they are important, but he focused on the founding period, and I began to understand then that Southern history encompassed more than the four-year fight for independence. My eyes had been opened. The Southern founding, the Jeffersonians, the postbellum South all became more interesting. I could see the South as a culturally distinct region with a four-hundred year history. It was America. That was Clyde's most important lesson.

Clyde has always wanted to write a book on the civilization of the South, similar to Jacob Burckhardt's "The Civilization of the Renaissance in Italy." He has an interest in the Southern people, black and white, that most don't see, particularly those who reduce the defense of the South to a latent desire to re-institute Jim Crow or slavery. That makes their straw man defense easier. Yet, if they bothered to truly *read* Clyde's work, they could not come to that conclusion. From John Smith to Walker Percy, Clyde has discussed, researched, written, and expounded upon all elements of Southern history and culture.

I had the benefit of working with Clyde on a regular basis. All of his students did. Most Southerners did not, at least not until the Internet allowed for the free exchange of ideas. The Abbeville Institute allows anyone to become his student, to read, to listen, to understand, to grow, to submerse themselves in the Southern tradition. It would not be the same without Clyde's decades of work. The South will survive because Clyde has left a trail of breadcrumbs for curious, intellectually honest people.

Alabama did eventually become my home. My wife is from Alabama and we live in "the heart of Dixie," but my education came from Carolina–Tar heel not Palmetto if Clyde has a say in it.

Clyde wrote me the other day apologizing for failing to send a couple of promised articles for the blog. He said that if he lives long enough, he'll write them next year.

You have too much work to do to die and too many Yankees to annoy by your continued existence. There are thousands of future students, eager minds like mine in 1997, that want to be your student, that want to know Southern culture and history, that want to be proud of their past and their heritage. You cannot let the Yankees win anytime soon.

Happy birthday, Clyde, from every student you have influenced in your life, either directly or indirectly, and many more to come.

Southern Conservatism and the "Gilded Age"

RUSSELL KIRK CALLED the early post-bellum period in American history the age of "Conservatism Frustrated." He lamented that the leading members of the conservative mind from 1865-1918 flirted with the radicalism of their compeers both before and during the Civil War and now were left with the daunting task of closing Pandora's Box, a Box they helped open:

> The New England reformers thought they had struck down evil incarnate when they crushed the Sable Genius of the South....They had dreaded an era of Jefferson Davis, but now they were in an era of Thaddeus Stevens, and of worse than Stevens. The merciless and vulgar old ironmaster, indeed, looked conspicuously admirable by the side of the Conklings and Mortons, the Butlers and Randalls, the Chandlers, Blaines, and Boutwells who scrabbled in the dust of a country blighted even worse spiritually than physically....They had been intent on abstract virtue, and now they awoke to find their fellow-Republicans, the oligarchs of their party, intent upon concrete plunder. The Mountain had yielded to the Directory.

It was North over South, and as Kirk wrote, "The obligations of conservative restoration therefore lay with the mind of the triumphant North; but the Northern intellect, which practically was the New England intellect, faltered before this enormous task." Kirk concluded that "By the time the First World War ended, true conservatism was nearly extinct in the United States, existing only in little circles of stubborn men who refused to be caught up in the expansive lust of their epoch...." Overall, "change," he wrote, "was preferred to continuity."

This is only partly true. Kirk's exemplary conservatives of the period, James Russell Lowell, E.L. Godkin, Henry Adams, and Brooks Adams, are part of the problem, and his lavish praise of the intellect of Henry Adams ignores the lasting vexation of the age, New England education, the product of what Thomas Jefferson famously called the "dark Federalist mills" of the North. Of course, Godkin, by Irish birth and education, can be excluded from the New England conservative school, and like William Graham Sumner was more correctly a classical liberal disgusted with corruption, democracy, centralization, imperialism, and cheap money, but he was a Northern partisan (though he had kind words to say for "Stonewall" Jackson), and a sharp critic of Southern culture.

Regardless, Kirk's choice for a chapter title is correct. Conservatism was frustrated in the late nineteenth century, but it was broader and more complex than his New England standards demonstrate. Arguably, this is the most important era for the student of the conservative mind. The dramatic changes in politics, government, and society induced by industrialization and egalitarianism presented problems for Western civilization and in particular the Western political and moral tradition. No one knew this better than Southern conservatives suffering under the Federal yoke, brow beaten and demonized by the conservatives Kirk praises for their rear-guard action against the forces Northerners helped unleash through their support for Abraham Lincoln and the Republican Party. American conservatism existed, not in little pockets as Kirk suggested, but down in Dixie.

James A. Bayard, the younger, of Delaware (arguably a Southern State in 1860) was one of these conservatives. Born into a prominent American family that counted among its members several U.S. Senators, war heroes during the American War for Independence, and a signatory to the United States Constitution, Bayard was as traditionally an American conservative as anyone in the antebellum United States. He was one of the lone voices against the Republican Party in the United States Senate during the War, a conservative working to maintain the Union of the founding generation, and a staunch opponent of centralization, democracy, and the executive usurpation of congressional power. Bayard fought against radical reconstruction and the political and social transformation of the United States in the years after the War. It was during this period that he displayed an open contempt for majority rule, reform, and modern education.

A common theme in Bayard's letters and speeches after the War centered on "Yankee Puritanism" and the combination of arbitrary power and moral reform. He feared a French Revolution on American soil and thought the Republican policies would surely lead to the same cataclysmic event in the United States. He called the Republican controlled Congress the "French directory" and complained how the "apathy of the people and their apparent ignorance or indifference" was leading to "the despotism which is advancing upon them." Temperance and reform were "dangerous to our future," and Bayard considered the reform movements of the day nothing short of the "demoralization" of the country.

Bayard made his last speech in the Senate in 1869 on the proposed Fifteenth Amendment to the Constitution, what he called the "Negro Suffrage" amendment. But Bayard did not focus his attack on race; rather, his was a blistering and calculated assault on universal suffrage, what he called the "hobby of the day." The Fifteenth Amendment, he said, would "subvert the system of government organized by our ancestors, and converts a confederated Republic into an elective despotism." He contended history showed that universal suffrage gave no "security for the preservation of civil liberty; and the imperial Government of France, with its six million majority, affords ample illustration of the inefficiency of such a remedy to secure liberty against the aggressions of power." He later wrote privately to his son, future Senator Thomas F. Bayard, Sr., that the amendment would be "the last drop in the cup which will cause the waters of bitterness to overflow."

Bayard believed that the American people, "at large have lost their capacity for self-government," and he thought the best men were shrinking from public life, leaving both the general and state governments in the hands of the "political traders." "Middle class government" had left Paris and London in a "shocking condition" and the only hope he had for America was "decentralization. It is by this alone," he said, "that a free govt of any kind can be preserved in so extended a country as ours with so heterogeneous a people." He later wrote, "there can be no empire in so extended a country as ours. Natural laws render it impossible even if Grant or his successor had the genius and capacity of Napoleon Bonaparte." Bayard would have agreed with John Tyler, Sr., who urged Thomas Jefferson in 1783 to reconsider turning down a seat in the Continental Congress. Tyler wrote, "I suppose your [reasons] are weighty, yet I would suggest that good and able men had better govern than be governed, since tis possible, indeed highly probable, that if the able and good withdraw themselves from society, the venal and ignorant will succeed."

"Demoralization," centralization, and "mediocrity," Bayard surmised, could be blamed squarely on the "Yankee school system" and the "surly press." "All periodical literature," he said, "written by half thinking men and the effect on the public is somewhat like the over gorging on food would be on the general health...." And poor education exacerbated the problem. The "Yankee school system" could "stimulate the brain, but it ignores mans [sic] moral nature and produces discontent with their condition among the masses…which can only end in anarchy and despotism." Because government had been handed to the masses, the people "were left to the control of trading politicians and the teachings of a licentious, sensational, and corrupt press." Bayard reflected that:

> what is called progress must be based on the moral culture of the people and not on merely intellectual excitement. That latter will end as it has been shown in New England in the decay of the thinking power and a more wide spread mental disturbance and ultimate extensive insanity. The whole doctrine of bringing all men to equality in mental moral or physical endowments by so called education is simply an absurdity. Equality of civil rights may be and is rational but equality is not the law of nature....

In his last years, Bayard prophesied that the "organized corruption of the monied class" and the popular press would ruin the United States, as it had other civilizations, and could only be arrested by "an honest sound state of opinion among our agricultural class." Ultimately, the modern press, whittled down by poor education and incapable men, would "weaken if not destroy its power or lead to too rigid a restriction of the public expression of opinion by some sort of censorship incompatible with republican institutions." Bayard linked agrarian interests with republicanism and a free, unregulated, and enlightened press with liberty. His position offered a traditional bulwark against a tidal wave of reform of modernity, and Bayard believed, as did his son, that the agrarian South exemplified the principles of 1776.

Richard Taylor of Louisiana displayed much of the same sentiments as Bayard in the post-bellum period. Taylor's lineage could be traced to the earliest settlers of Virginia; his grandfather was a colonel in the Continental Army during the American War for Independence, and his father, Zachary Taylor, was one of the most distinguished general officers in American history and later President of the United States. Like Bayard, Taylor was a disinterested statesman cut from the cloth of old American principles. His cause in 1861 as a Confederate general was the same as Washington's and Jefferson's in 1776. To men like Bayard and Taylor, the South was the continuity between the founding generation and their own, and after the War, Taylor waged a rearguard action against the fanaticism of so-called Northern conservatives. To him and conservative men of the South, losing meant the destruction rather than the preservation of the Union and the founding tradition. His memoirs titled *Destruction and Reconstruction* highlight post-bellum Southern conservative thought.

Taylor's response at the conclusion of the War to a recent German emigrant turned Union soldier outlined his understanding of history and traditional American principles, principles the South defended and exemplified. This unnamed German "comforted" Taylor "by assurances that we of the South would speedily recognize our ignorance and errors, especially about slavery and the rights of States, and rejoice in the results of the war." Taylor apologized "meekly" for his "ignorance, on the ground that my ancestors had come from England to Virginia in 1608, and, in the short intervening period of two-hundred and fifty odd years, had found no time to transmit to me correct ideas of the duties of American citizenship." The German smiled and offered to instruct Taylor whenever needed. This was not "Yankee education" at work, but recent German immigrants—many of whom were Northern partisans disaffected by their failures in the communist revolutions of 1848—influenced American social policy after the War. Radical transformations in public education and the kindergarten movement are the most conspicuous examples, and Northern agitators clung to such education "reform" with both hands.

Taylor described Washington D.C. shortly after the War as little better than Sodom. Paroled Union officers "gorged with loot" taken from Southern homes flaunted their new found treasure, mostly in the form of lavish gifts to their women. The city swarmed with prostitutes who freely conducted business in the shadow of the executive mansion. This was not the Union or the capital city his father and his grandfather had known. Lust for power had supplanted republican principles. And the political class exacerbated the situation.

As a former Whig with political connections through his father, Taylor had access to the leading men of the Republican Party after the War, most of whom were former Northern Whigs. Taylor described "The Great Commoner" Thad Stevens of Pennsylvania as a frank man with little remorse for the Southern people—Taylor feared Stevens hoped to stretch his neck. Stevens declared without reservation that the Union of the founders was dead and called the Constitution a "worthless bit of old parchment." In his estimation, the South had to be kept from power else they would align with the "Copperheads" of the North and wreck the true agenda of the War, the radical transformation of America.

Taylor thought President Andrew Johnson attempted to keep the barbarians at bay, and though he had little regard for the President, Taylor considered Johnson's attempt to keep the office above the wretched rent seekers, bully politicians, and radical reformers to be at least admirable. Taylor remarked that he was disappointed to know that the restoration of the old Union was never contemplated by the Republican leadership. He believed, he said naively, that the War was for the restoration of the Union and that the old order would be at least maintained in the North. He now knew otherwise.

Even men who would later be viewed as statesmen turned their backs on the founding tradition. Taylor thought Charles Sumner of Massachusetts, doubtless more anti-Southern than anyone in Washington after taking a beating from

Preston Brooks, to be an educated man, refined and cultured, and open to logic and reason. Not so he discovered. Taylor recounted how Sumner "seemed to be over-educated—had retained, not digested his learning; and beautiful flowers of literature were attached to him by filaments of memory, as lovely orchids to sapless sticks. Hence he failed to understand the force of language, and became the victim of his own metaphors, mistaking them for facts. He had the irritable vanity and weak nerves of a woman, and was bold to rashness in speculation, destitute as he was of the ordinary masculine sense of responsibility." Bayard had simply called Sumner a "pompous ass" when the two had sparred in the Senate. Both descriptions fit. Sumner personified "Yankee education."

Taylor eventually gave up trying to influence policy and spent several years in Europe. American politics had been given to demagogues, banks, and rent seekers, what Bayard called the "monied class." Taylor agreed. He could find few reasons to hope and even mourned that the South was succumbing to the poison brought to it by the War. The only hope was tradition, the same tradition that Kirk sought in Northern voices. Taylor saw it in the South and in the founding generation. "Respect for the memories and deeds of our ancestors is security for the present, seed-corn for the future..." he wrote. Yet, he feared it was already lost by the 1870s. "The story of six centuries of sturdy effort by which our English forefathers wrought out their liberties is unknown, certainly unappreciated. Even the struggles of our grandfathers are forgotten, and the names of Washington, Adams, Hamilton, Jay, Marshall, Madison, and Story awaken no fresher memories in our minds, no deeper emotions in our hearts, than do those of Solon, Leonidas, and Pericles." Taylor was prophetic, for in 2014 most Americans would be hard pressed to recognize even the American names on his list.

Such melancholy aligns with Kirk's description of the period, but Taylor had hope, and he concluded his memoir with words that should make any conservative take notice.

> Traditions are mighty influences in restraining peoples. The light that reaches us from above takes countless ages to traverse the awful chasm separating us from its parent star; yet it comes straight and true to our eyes, because each tender wavelet is linked to the other, receiving and transmitting the luminous rays. Once break the continuity of the stream, and men will deny its heavenly origin, and seek its source in the feeble glimmer of earthy corruption.

Respect for tradition could still be found among the majority of Southerners in the Gilded Age. Kirk cannot be faulted for underestimating them. Southerners were marginalized and maligned by the stigma of the War and secession and were being emasculated by Northern interests and Northern dogma. Nevertheless Southerners, not the Adams family of Massachusetts, should be the focus of study for historians looking for "true conservatism" in this period. They were and are the "security" and the "seed-corn" for future generations and a lasting echo of the American tradition that dates to the earliest settlements in Virginia.

People Along the Way: Dan Smoot

DAN SMOOT NEVER CONSIDERED himself to be a Southern conservative, though he was born and reared in Missouri and spent his early adult life in Texas. He was one of the leading conservative voices in the 1960s and hosted a weekly television program titled "The Dan Smoot Report."

There were once principled men who were willing to carry the conservative standard against seemingly insurmountable odds, even if it meant public ridicule. Smoot was one of those men, and his brand of conservatism was heavily influenced by his time in the South. The giants of conservatism in the post-World War II era–Russell Kirk, Richard Weaver, Henry Regnery, James Kilpatrick, Mel Bradford, et. al.,–understood that much of American conservatism was nurtured in the soil of the South, a region that was slow to adopt the consumerism and multinationalism of the mainstream Republican Party. Country club Republicans and their neoconservative allies eventually purged these men from respectable public discourse. America has suffered as a result.

Smoot's autobiography *People Along the Way* contains interesting tidbits about life in the Great Depression South, among them the common interaction among white and black Southerners. These stories would not be considered politically correct, nor would they be presented by the modern historical profession. They involve everyday white and black Southerners interacting without a hint of racial animosity or spite.

For example, Smoot was a tramp in his late teens, living in "hobo jungles" moving from town to town along the rails looking for work during the lean years of the early depression. He was instructed not to venture into the South by other vagrants. Why? Because the only hobos who could get a helping hand in the

South were black. "Down there," said one hobo, "Negroes could get help and preferential treatment from white folks, who would not give anything but the back of the hand to a white boy like me who was not born and raised there." Smoot ventured to the South anyway and found Texas to be a paradise. The people were friendly, the weather warm, and everyone was willing to help the poor boy with ripped clothes, worn-out shoes, and a dirty face. Southern hospitality benefitted both races during the Depression.

Smoot also recounted a time he spent picking cotton to earn a nickel. He didn't last long on the job because he couldn't do it as well as the black folks who "thoroughly enjoyed" the activity. Smoot described how the black community viewed cotton picking time as a holiday around Dallas. "They would give up jobs, business, almost anything, to be in the cotton patch for the star of picking season. Every year, companies hiring lots of Negroes, and families dependent upon them for domestic help, were hard hit by unannounced mass exertions of Negroes 'gone to the cotton patch.'"

His time was much different:

> For days I crawled through a field, dragging a cotton sack, picking one row of cotton, alongside a big Negro picking two rows at a time, dragging a sack more than twice the size of mine, cleaning two rows faster and better than I cleaned one. A man of infinite jest, he entertained me, himself, and everyone within ten cotton rows of us, by teasing me about stuffing me into his cotton sack, getting me sneaked in and weighed in as part of his picked cotton, then helping me escape so we could do it all over again all day long. He would pay me half of what he got paid for my weight. We would thus get rich; he, doing all the work; I, doing nothing but loll around in his cotton sack, or rest covered up by cotton in the wagon, waiting to escape.

Smoot then reflected how he would think of that man and the cotton picking festivals years later when "after Eleanor Roosevelt had made it a fashion among compassionate northerners to grieve over the plight of Negroes 'in the southern states,' where one of the many atrocities imposed upon them was being forced to crawl all day on their hands and knees, picking cotton under the broiling sun."

Smoot described the black communities in 1930s Dallas as well maintained and orderly populated by hard working people with strong families. This does not fit the current "New South" narrative.

Smoot eventually fell in love in Texas and married a native Texian. His portrayal of pre-1960s feminist women would be considered archaic, but it provides a perspective on "women's rights" long ago lost in the rush to "equalize" men and women. Remember, he was mostly among young Southern women as a teenager:

> Now, in my old age, having seen what I have seen, I am most grateful to God that, in the parts of American where I lived as a teenager, the girls I became acquainted with were performing the role that girls and young women must perform in a civilized society: maintaining for themselves, and enforcing upon boys and men, high standards of sexual morality. Inasmuch as God made males the sexual aggressors, and inasmuch as sexual desire is the most powerful of all human passions, there is only one human agency that can keep society from destroying itself by mindless, degenerate promiscuity: that agency is a high level of sexual morality in women, and, by women, enforced upon men. Too bad that feminists and civil-righters today are dragging women down from their preeminently important, God-given role as keepers of the flame of civilization trying to make women as low as men!

This is not some bombastic, misogynistic screed, but a carefully reasoned plea for a return to life when women had *more* power than they possess today, even in a "liberated" society. He always considered his wife to be mentally superior, and he believed in strong women. But to Smoot, "strong" was in the sense that women were the morally superior vessels of life, the gatekeepers to proper civilization who could tame men. Smoot believed that, like Augusta Jane Evans's Edna Earl in *St. Elmo*, it was a woman's job to ensure that proper civilization survived. Men left to their devices would degenerate into irresponsible, lazy hobos without the soft but firm hand of feminine morality.

Smoot's parents were sharecroppers. At one point, his father moved the family to La Forge, Missouri were he was the only white man to work a former cotton plantation. "Descendants of whites who had owned it before the War, owned it in the 1920s; and descendants of Negroes who had worked it as slaves, lived on it in the 1920s and, as free hired hands, worked all but our little sharecropped part of it." They were poor–thought he said he never felt that way because there were always poorer people around him–but Smoot enjoyed his time living in log cabins, jaunting through the woods or along the Mississippi River, or harvest festivals and cattle roundups. He read the classics, got a small taste of formal education ,and lived the agrarian life as a boy. It taught him independence.

Smoot eventually went to law school and quit, obtained a graduate degree in American studies, joined the FBI (and quit or was fired depending on whom you believe) and became one of the most outspoken conservatives of his day. He once said "an existence without risk is an existence of little worth." Perhaps this is more true today than in his time with militant political correctness running America and the Southern tradition at even greater risk than when Richard Weaver wrote his famous dissertation *The Southern Tradition at Bay.*

Smoot may not have been the typically Southern man, but it was the South that cut his teeth. Below are two clips from his now infamous Dan Smoot Report and one speech he gave in the 1960s. That speech is important for his perspective on "totalitarian liberals," apathetic rich conservatives, and the hard-working Americans who tended to support his views. Here is the Southern political tradition in full display. If we could only have some of our giants back....

JEFFERSON DAVIS AND THE LAME LION OF LYNCHBURG

SENATOR JOHN WARWICK DANIEL (1842-1910) of Lynchburg, Virginia was a gentleman's gentleman. Daniel served in the U.S. Senate from 1887 until his death in 1910 and was known as "The Lame Lion of Lynchburg" after being severely wounded in the War for Southern Independence. He was shot through the hip at First Manassas and struggled off the battlefield using two rifles for crutches. He removed a bullet from his hand with a pocketknife during the defense of Richmond in 1862, and he was permanently disabled after trying to rally his men at the Battle of the Wilderness in 1864. He nearly bled to death. His political career was marked by the same staunch defense of the South and State's rights. One contemporary remarked:

> I fancy that John Daniel would have named Thomas Jefferson as the greatest American statesman; certainly his own political instincts and ideals were largely those which Jefferson had caused to prevail. Like Jefferson, he trusted the people of his country, because by close intimacy and wide experience he had found them worthy of trust and believed them also worthy of freedom and political power. His abiding faith in the honesty of his fellow citizens, his rooted belief in their common sense, his trust in the appeal to the educated reason of the voters, his assurance that human society is capable of indefinite advancement in virtue and uprightness, his firm conviction that majorities rule not by might alone but of right as well, made of Thomas Jefferson the typical American and the like qualities made of John Daniel the typical Jeffersonian Democrat.

Part III: Southern Comfort

Daniel lived in a time when Southern men and women were required to understand the lives and character of Confederate heroes and to do so publicly. Senator Sam Ervin of North Carolina had a humorous story about this in 1973; fully 100 years after the War, Ervin recounts, Southerners were expected to know their history. Such is not the case today. Any whiff of an attachment to Confederate leaders or the traditional South means certain political death, even in Dixie it seems.

Daniel was asked to speak about Jefferson Davis's life and character before the Virginia Legislature in 1890, just one year after the former President's death. His purpose was to honor the man and his legacy and to vindicate the South and its struggle for independence. Daniel said, "Jefferson Davis never advocated an idea that did not have its foundation in the Declaration of Independence; that was not deducible from the Constitution of the United States as the fathers who made it interpreted its meaning; that had not been rung in his ears and stamped upon his heart from the hour when his father baptized him in the name of Jefferson and he first saw the light in a Commonwealth (Kentucky) that was yet vocal with the States'-Rights Resolutions of 1798." Davis, Daniel insisted, should have been etched in stone among the great pantheon of world heroes. His cause was that of America.

Daniel asked, "Did not the South love American institutions? What schoolboy cannot tell? Who wrote the great Declaration? Who threw down the gage, "Liberty or Death?" Who was chief framer of the Constitution? Who became its great expounder? Who wrote the Bill of Rights which is copied far and wide by free commonwealths? Who presided over the convention that made the Constitution and became in field and council its all in all defender? Jefferson, Henry, Madison, Marshall, Mason, Washington, speak from your graves and give the answer."

And Daniel emphasized that American history had been defined by the South, from the Old Northwest territory to Texas, Southerners had led the charge to settle North America, to bring America to the West, and by America he meant the principles that defined the South: liberty, independence, and free government. Their cause was that of the patriot who rode to battle against the British in 1776, both North and South.

Daniel believed, somewhat optimistically, that in the future the American people would remember Jefferson Davis as a hero rather than a traitor. All signs pointed in that direction in 1890. Lee and Jackson were considered American heroes. Davis resisted the charge for secession in the months prior to Mississippi withdrawing from the Union in 1861, and his farewell address to the Senate was considered to be one of the most eloquent and beautiful in American history.

He loved the Union and he loved America, no less so than Abraham Lincoln, perhaps even more deeply. Daniel, of course, could not see the tornado of political correctness that would eventually dislodge free thought and free speech from the foundation of American discourse.

In the same year, 1890, Daniel edited and published a substantial book on Davis titled *Life and Reminiscences of Jefferson Davis*. He dedicated it to, "THE PEOPLE OF THE SOUTH TO YOU IS DEDICATED THIS MEMORIAL VOLUME OF YOUR HONORED AND MUCH LOVED CHIEFTAIN JEFFERSON DAVIS, THE STATESMAN, SOLDIER, AND CHRISTIAN, IN WHOM WAS EMBODIED AS IN NO OTHER MAN THE POLITICAL VIEWS AND SENTIMENTS, WHICH YOU SO ABLY MAINTAINED IN THAT MEMORABLE CONFLICT OF 1861-65." Over half the tome contains contemporary accounts of Davis as a man, a statesman, and an American.

Daniel introduced the book with a sentence that still rings true one-hundred and twenty-four years later, "Jefferson Davis has been more misrepresented, and is to-day more misunderstood by many than any character that figured in the Civil War of 1861 to 1864 [sic]." Daniel thought this was the result of Davis's character, most importantly his refusal to ask for a pardon after the War. Yet, he considered Davis to be "one of the purest and bravest of the public men which our country has produced;—that he was an honest, able and clear thinker, and a true seeker for the good of humanity. He was the incarnation of the Southern cause." It would only be natural, Daniel opined, for Americans to see his importance. Had not lesser men been vindicated by time?

Daniel argued Davis exemplified everything America stood for, both past and present. "The character of Jefferson Davis," Daniel wrote, "will grow, in the general estimate. Scholars will ponder it, and will bring to the light the facts which have been neglected or ignored; and statesmen who have been under the spur of interest to paint him darkly, will feel that impulse to do justice which springs up from a sense of injustice done. A ripe scholar, a vigorous writer, a splendid orator, a brave soldier, a true gentleman, an accomplished statesman, a sturdy champion, a proud, pure patriot, a lover of liberty, a hero: this is the Jefferson Davis that history will cherish."

Davis and the South lost the War, but would not Washington, Jefferson, Madison, Rutledge, Marion, Macon, Taylor, Mason, Henry and other Southerners suffer the fate of their Confederate descendants had they lost the War for American Independence? Would Americans reduce their glory and place Gage, Cornwallis, and George III above their honor? The heroes who waged a war for the "Principles of '76" shared a common cause with the patriots of 1861, and on Jefferson Davis's birthday, all Southerners, nay all Americans, should remember that fact. Daniel was simply speaking the truth. After all, he had bled for it, and his body had been shattered defending it. Davis nearly rotted to death in prison after the War facing charges for a crime he did not commit, treason. The truth set him free and vindicated his cause. The truth led the Lame Lion of Lynchburg to honor his former President. The truth led millions of Southerners to defend Davis, even into the late 20th century. That doesn't mean much today, but it should.

The Tuckers of Virginia

IF ANY AMERICAN TODAY were to listen to the nationalists in charge of either the political class or American education at large, they would get the sense that it is settled science that the American Union is comprised of one people held together by a national government with uncontested sovereignty over all matters foreign and domestic. Certainly, States and local governments can make laws, but those laws are subject to review by the national judiciary and can be declared invalid at any time if a national judge rules that the law in question violates the prevailing national opinion in regard to any matter, political, social, or economic. Not even national laws crafted by the national legislature can stop the black robed federal adjudicators.

It has not always been this way. There are hundreds of dusty tomes buried deep in both research and public libraries that expose this position as a fraud, at least in regard to the federal American system as designed by the founding generation. And not all lawyers, legal scholars, or judges used to be corrupted by nationalist propaganda. There were hearty souls who effectively refuted the nationalist lie made popular by Alexander Hamilton, John Marshall, Joseph Story, Daniel Webster, and Abraham Lincoln. Many of these works are available for free online, but knowing who to look for and where to look can be a daunting task. Finding quotations on the Constitution by any of the nationalists is a simple web search away, but their opponents have been relegated to the dark corners of acceptable thought, tarnished with charges of treason or worse. Most of them are Southern. This makes their ideas—long considered outmoded or frankly dead by the modern academy—not only dangerous to the political class and the ruling establishment, but politically incorrect.

This is unjust and thousands (hopefully millions) of Americans are finally realizing that the American federal republic as crafted does not mesh with the political monstrosity on the banks of the Potomac River today. The "federal" leviathan a cancer, the very thing most in the founding generation wished to avoid and diligently argued would never happen even if the Constitution were ratified in 1788. It wouldn't have been had anyone listened to the real "federalists" of the antebellum period, namely those who believed in a federated republic of independent States held together in a Union for expressly delegated purposes outlined in a Constitution of limited powers. There were exponents of this position North and South in 1788. A compelling case could be made that every *proponent* of the Constitution accepted this position during the State ratifying conventions, including the arch-nationalists James Wilson of Pennsylvania and Hamilton of New York. What happened after the Constitution was adopted is another story, but no family held more firmly to the argument that the Constitution was, and is, a compact between independent States with expressly delegated powers than the Tucker family of Virginia. They deserve our attention and thus a weeklong focus on their political, social, and constitutional beliefs.

Starting today, the Abbeville Review and the Clyde Wilson Library will feature pieces written by or on the Tuckers. The first great constitutional scholar of the family, St. George Tucker, is the focus of Clyde Wilson's piece on Monday at the Clyde Wilson Library. St. George Tucker wrote the first comprehensive study of the Constitution after its adoption as a corollary to Blackstone's famous commentaries on English law. His edition of Blackstone was widely read and used in legal studies for much of antebellum American history. St. George Tucker was friends with Thomas Jefferson and a true republican of the old Virginia order. His *View of the Constitution of the United States* should be standard reading for anyone interested in a detailed examination of the "compact fact" of the Constitution, perhaps even more so than John Taylor's *New Views on the Constitution of the United States*, a study written in response to John Adams's highly centralized exposition on American constitutionalism.

Tuesday's piece is written by St. George Tucker's oldest son, Henry St. George Tucker. Henry St. George Tucker was appointed to the law faculty for both the College of William and Mary and the University of Virginia. He served as a member of Congress, as the president of the Virginia Supreme Court of Appeals, and less conspicuously as a captain in the War of 1812. He was a prominent member of the second generation of Americans, reared in the Virginia republican tradition and a staunch defender of originalism. His piece comes from his 1843 *Lectures on Constitutional Law* and is a well-argued attack on the "one people" thesis of early American history. He expertly shows that an "American people" has never existed and that the colonies, far from being an amorphous mass of land under the singular direction of the crown, shared no allegiance to one another nor did any colonial American think of an American "nation" or an American "people."

Wednesday's essay is by St. George Tucker's second son, Nathaniel Beverley Tucker, better known as a writer of fiction than for his essays on the Constitution or political philosophy. His *The Partisan Leader* was highly influential among Southern secessionists, particularly in the 1850s, and Edgar Allen Poe called Tucker's lesser known novel *George Balcome* "the *best* American novel" in an 1837 review in *The Southern Literary Messenger*. Beverley Tucker also served as a member of the law faculty at the College of William and Mary and counted among his contacts some of the most important men in the Union, among them President John Tyler and Secretary of State Abel P. Upshur. His 1839 treatise *A Discourse on the Genius of the Federative System of the United States* reprinted by the Abbeville Review is a call for the men of Virginia to lead a renaissance of federalism in America, for Tucker rightly expresses his belief in the "compact fact" of the Constitution. It was Virginia that birthed Washington, Jefferson, Madison, Henry, and a host of other great Americans. To Tucker, it made sense that Virginia would be at the vanguard of a renewed call for real federalism.

Henry St. George Tucker's son, John Randolph Tucker, authored the Thursday piece at the Abbeville Review, an 1887 commencement address delivered at South Carolina College (University of South Carolina) titled *The Old and the New South*. J.R. Tucker was Attorney General for Virginia both before and during the War for Southern Independence and member of the United States Congress after the War. His address is not only a sweeping history of the antebellum period, the causes of the War, and the ramifications of Southern defeat, but a clarion call for Southerners to defend their heritage and the principles for which the South bled during the War, namely the original understanding of the Constitution as outlined by John C. Calhoun, a personal friend of Tucker's.

The final installment of Tucker week is by Henry St. George Tucker III, John Randolph Tucker's only son. Henry St. George Tucker III was a member of Congress, the president of the American Bar Association and the Dean of the Law School at Washington and Lee University and George Washington University. His 1927 essay is a thorough shredding of the expansion of the "General Welfare Clause" made famous by Joseph Story's commentaries on the Constitution. No one has surpassed Tucker's clarity of argument either before or after his essay was written.

It must be noted that each of the Tucker's were not only great legal scholars, they were devout Christians. That is apparent in their writing. Several of the Virginia Tuckers later served as men of the cloth, with Beverly Dandridge Tucker

(1846-1930)—nephew of John Randolph Tucker—appointed as the Bishop of the Episcopal Diocese of Southern Virginia. His sons would be prominent members of the Episcopal Church. Son Henry St. George Tucker would be the presiding Bishop for the American Episcopal Church (1938-1946) and another son, Francis Bland Tucker, was a famous composer and Rector of Christ Church in Savannah, Georgia until his death in 1984.

All five pieces in our Tucker week are scholarly. They are meant to be chewed and digested, read and re-read, and hopefully serve to whet the appetite for more research into this important Virginia family. They provide enough intellectual ammunition to destroy any nationalist argument. The Tuckers are a true American legal and ecclesiastical dynasty in need a Requiem Mass. Their work, not that of Story or Marshall, should be required reading for American legal scholars. That can start here.

Fire Cured Dark Leaf

COTTON AND TOBACCO. For years those two agricultural products were as synonymous with the South as sweet tea and grits. Cotton still is, but tobacco has fallen out of favor, though Southerners still love it and use tobacco products in greater numbers per capita than any other people in America.

Tobacco, not cotton, was king in Virginia throughout much of its history. Virginians settled debts with the weed and every important Virginian in the founding generation grew tobacco. It was a staple of life, the major source of economic gain in the tidewater region of the State, and a source of great pain when the plant wore out the soil. Tobacco led John Taylor of Caroline to write the first American treatise on agriculture, *Arator*, in 1813. Tobacco allowed the Virginia gentry to develop into the greatest political class America has known. Perhaps that is partly why modern progressives hate it. "Big Tobacco" is synonymous with racism, slavery, poor health, and white manism. Expunge tobacco from American history and the greatest generation in American history—early federal Virginia farmers—are relegated to the dustbin of the past, if they are not already.

The plant also partially led to the development of the so-called "New South," this time through the manufacture of chewing tobacco and machine rolled cigarettes. C. Vann Woodward argued in his *Origins of the New South* that men like Richard J. Reynolds, James B. Duke, and William T. Blackwell personified the dichotomy between the Old South and the New. To Woodward, these men were as much progressive captains of industry as their Northern counterparts in New York or Boston. This is one of many things he got wrong. These tobacco entrepreneurs made millions, but each man was rooted in the Southern tradition. Tobacco came from the earth, the farm, and the South, and they all knew it. The tobacco industry is more accurately the continuity between the Old South and the New, if such a thing existed until the late 20th century. When men are still more interested in the auction price of bright leaf than the stock ticker at Wall Street, the Old South still lives.

The tobacco industry employed thousands of Southerners, both white and black, even at the height of Jim Crow in the 1890s. One recent historian complained that Richard Reynolds did not do enough to alleviate racial strife in the South, nor did he advocate for black Southerners, many of whom worked in his factories. That says it all. Reynolds could have refused to employ blacks, but simply by providing jobs and allowing them to leave the shackles of sharecropping was a vast economic improvement. And both James B. Duke and his father, George Washington Duke, were revered in the black community for their philanthropy around Durham, North Carolina. The American Tobacco Company, led by the Duke family, was perhaps the first American "monopoly," and the money that poured into North Carolina led to improvements in education, public works, and jobs. "Big tobacco" did that. Blackwell's "Bull Durham" tobacco brand took off after the War because Yankees stole much of his product when they sacked Durham in 1865. After they went back North, they kept requesting it. They could only stuff so much in their pockets. Now, Blackwell was stuffing his with Yankee greenbacks.

Incidentally, Washington Duke had opposed slavery before the War and was conscripted into the Confederate Navy. Richard Reynolds was too young to serve, but his brother did, and according to family lore, young Richard hid the family horses from the invading Yankees near the end of the War. "Big tobacco," like other Southern industries, found its origins in the Confederate experience, or more accurately the Southern experience. For most of American history, anything worthwhile in American culture was synonymous with Southern culture. That only changed after the War.

At the very least, Southerners should appreciate the contributions tobacco has made to the South, both before and after the War. After all, America, the real America of Jefferson, Washington, Madison, Henry, and the birth of real republicanism and American culture in Virginia, had its roots in fire-cured dark leaf. Indeed, the first permanent English colony in America, Jamestown, would not have survived without it.

Tobacco farms are slowly fading in the South. Kentucky still has several large operations, as does Maryland, North Carolina, and Virginia, but nowhere near the number that existed even half-a-century ago. No one any longer disputes that tobacco is unhealthy, but there has always been a certain American allure to the product. It was long considered masculine to use tobacco and still is among cigar smokers. Yet even that industry is now under attack.

Since the 1990s, Americans, Southerners included, have been lining up to sue the tobacco industry. Just look at the $23 billion an Escambia County, Florida jury recently awarded to the widow of a life-long smoker. He didn't know cigarettes were harmful. And Grant was a better general than Lee. Or perhaps he missed the 1604 memo from King James on the harmful effects of smoking, from yellow teeth and bad breath, to chronic coughing and disease of the brain. Maybe that document could be used by tobacco company attorneys as evidence for the known health dangers. It's only been around for four hundred years. Of course, "Big Tobacco" has deep pockets and lawyers love to litigate. It isn't their money. We know it's bad, but as Jerry Reed sang, many just say "I'll have another puff."

Confederate Coca-Cola

TODAY (JULY 8) is Lt. Col. John Stith Pemberton's birthday. While not as important to the Confederacy as John C. Pemberton, John Stith Pemberton contributed more to American culture and to the image of the New South than virtually any man who donned the gray during the War for Southern Independence.

Pemberton studied medicine at the Reform Medical College of Georgia in Macon and was graduated in 1850 at the age of 19. Five years later he established a pharmacy in Columbus, Georgia, then a bustling industrial town at the fall-line on the Chattahoochee River. By 1860, his lab on Broad Street contained over $35,000 in equipment and he marketed his business as a company dedicated to "manufacturing all the pharmaceutical and chemical preparations used in the arts and sciences." This included perfume. The ladies of Columbus loved to buy his aromatic concoctions.

Then the War came. Pemberton did not march out with the Columbus Guards in 1861. Only a handful of those men came home. He spent the War like many residents in Columbus, contributing to the War effort through industry. Columbus was the second most important industrial city in the South and manufactured everything from uniforms, rain cloth, boots, and buttons, to munitions, bagging, barrels, and iron, including the unfinished Confederate ram the C.S.S. *Jackson*.

This was not lost on the Union army. Columbus was targeted by the Yankees in the final months of the War as part of their total war strategy. General James Harrison Wilson hammered through Alabama in 1865, leaving behind a swath of destruction that rivaled that of Sherman's march to and from the sea in Georgia and South Carolina.

Part III: Southern Comfort

On April 16, 1865 (Easter Sunday), the Union Army appeared on the Alabama side of the Chattahoochee. All able bodied men (and boys) in Alabama (modern day Phenix City) and Columbus readied to defend the city. Pemberton was a lieutenant colonel in the Third Georgia Cavalry Battalion (Home Guard) and bravely faced the occupying army the night of the battle. He was slashed across the chest in the action and almost died from his wounds. Columbus was burned the next day, and like Columbia, South Carolina, after the city surrendered.

Pemberton spent the next year recovering from his wounds, and in the process he became addicted to opium. He put his pharmacy to work looking to find a way to ease his pain without the drug. By 1866, he had produced a product he later called Pemberton's French Wine Coca, an alcoholic drink that probably contained a trace of cocaine.

When Pemberton moved to Atlanta in 1870, he brought his medicinal recipe with him and marketed it as a cure for several ailments, but in particular as a cure for opium addition. Again, upper class women became his primary customers. Laudanum was a commonly prescribed drug in the nineteenth century for headaches and was highly addictive. Pemberton's French Wine Coca promised relief without the painful withdraw symptoms of opiates. Pemberton's career had taken off. He became a trustee of the Atlanta Medical College, later Emory University School of Medicine, and had a business in Philadelphia, Pennsylvania that manufactured and marketed his pharmaceuticals.

When Atlanta went dry in the 1880s, Pemberton was forced to find an alternative to his alcoholic product. While mixing a batch one day he stumbled upon what later became known as Coca-Cola, a mix of the coca syrup (absent the cocaine) and carbonated water. Coca-cola the soft drink was born, but the formula had not changed much since Pemberton first mixed it in Columbus in 1866 as a suffering Confederate veteran.

Pemberton believed that his new non-alcoholic drink–what he marketed as the "ideal temperance drink"–would eventually become a "national drink," and so in 1887 he incorporated the Coca-Cola Company and let his only son Charles, also an opium addict, run the company. Pemberton died less than a year later of stomach cancer, broke and still helplessly addicted to opium. Just before he died, however, his son persuaded him to sell the company to Asa Chandler for $550. Chandler later made millions on the drink, as did Ernest Woodruff, a businessman from Pemberton's final resting place, Columbus, GA. Pemberton's son also later died from complications related to opium addiction without a dime to show from his father's formula.

Yet, without the War and the Battle of Columbus in 1865, the world may never have been introduced to Coca-Cola, or by default RC Cola and Ne-hi, both invented by Columbus grocer Claud Hatcher after he refused to pay high prices for Coke syrup. Perhaps more than any other drink, Coke and cola beverages are synonymous with the South and originated with Southern ingenuity (Pepsi was developed in North Carolina). So, the next time you tip a glass of your favorite carbonated cola drink, remember that Yankees didn't invent any of them and what is now considered an "American" drink originated in the South. Such is the case with most of the so-called "American" cultural icons.

A Black Armband for Southern Education

THOMAS JEFFERSON FOUNDED the University of Virginia in an effort to combat the "dark Federalist mills of the North" and keep Virginians home for their higher education. He was not alone in this endeavor. It had been customary for Southerners to travel north or to Europe for their advanced degrees, but by the middle of the nineteenth century, several institutions of higher education had been established in the Southern states and all featured rigorous academic standards that rivaled their Northern counterparts.

Most of the men who served in these institutions picked up the sword to defend the South in 1861. The entire student body at several Southern institutions enrolled in the Confederate army. Southern higher education and the defense of the South, both physically and intellectually, were synonymous for many years after the War ended. Two small liberal arts colleges stood above the rest in this regard: The University of the South and Washington and Lee University. The University of the South maintained a strict devotion to Southern principles after the War and Robert E. Lee served as president of what became Washington and Lee University from 1865 until his death.

Yet, no one should be surprised by the recent turn of events at Washington and Lee. It has happened before. By the late 1990s, The University of the South had changed its name—Sewanee—had removed Confederate symbols from its All Saints Chapel, had "lost" its ceremonial baton which featured images of the Confederacy, and had abolished several traditions, most importantly the strict dress code for both students and faculty. A university founded in part by Confederate General Leonidas Polk with the express purpose of distancing higher education from Northern influences had caved to...Northern influences, or more properly the distortion of history and culture by "those people" as Lee called them.

This is a trend that has accelerated in recent years. Every name, custom, or emblem linking a college or university to its antebellum Southern past is under assault. College is a multi-million dollar business driven by enrollment and "inclusion." University presidents get better jobs or bigger paychecks when they can point to buildings, endowments, and enrollment growth during their tenure. See current Washington and Lee President Kenneth P. Ruscio's "accomplishments" at the school. Many of the most prestigious Southern institutions have become homes for carpetbag presidents with little understanding of the South, Southern culture, or Southern education. They look at the South as a series of backwater provinces ready to be enlightened by their superior intellect.

Sadly, even many Southern "academics" clamor to prove how backward their section was (and is) and how its remembered past has been wrong since the beginning. These Southern academics are so eager for recognition and acceptance by the American collective, i.e. acceptable opinion, that they readily distance themselves from the "sins" of their ancestors. Quite simply, they argue, Southerners lie. In their mind, Southern history is filled with "myths" and embellishments designed to sweep away or veil the ugly truth of the Southern mind. The post-bellum accounts of the War, secession, and Southern history were blatant revisionism designed to soften the blow of Reconstruction and hasten inclusion in American society. Southerners, then, are little more than disingenuous fools who need "reconstructed" intellectuals to help them understand their "true" history.

"Southern Studies" programs are in large part responsible for this trend. While often housed in university history departments, their proper home should behavioral science. Southerners are specimens to be dissected under a microscope, lab rats given cheese and electric shocks to determine behavior, and they, unlike their Northern masters, are predictably animalistic in their routines, driven only by lust, hate, and greed. See for example the Thomas Jefferson/Sally Hemings "affair" now considered historical fact, or a thesis from a graduate student at the University of Delaware on the grand Louisiana Belle Grove plantation where he assumes, with no evidentiary support, that the reason the large hospital for slaves was located near the main home was to intimidate and show the majesty of the "master class." You see, Southerners cannot be humane. There had to be some insidious reason for providing medical care for sick and wounded African-Americans.

The mainstream academy has been lost for years, and the Washington and Lee fiasco is simply more proof that even historic Southern colleges are destined to capitulate to tide of fashionable opinion. Higher education stopped being about education and the free exchange of ideas many years ago. Endowments, new buildings, administrative salaries, and athletic programs drive university decisions and budgets. Kenneth Ruscio obviously calculated that his decision to remove the flags from Lee's tomb will increase enrollment and fill the university coffers. Thus, like most conclusions drawn by carpetbaggers, it was not based on "diversity," or even history and tradition, but money. Washington and Lee can now claim they have exorcised their Confederate demons and have caught up with the times. This won't stop. The only solution is to do what Jefferson, Polk, and others did in their quest to preserve the culture and education of their communities in the antebellum South: found new institutions and ignore the old. It is only in this way that the South can be saved. The Abbeville Institute is part of that process.

Jefferson Davis and the Kenner Mission

A FEW MONTHS BACK, I had a student ask me about Don Livingston's characterization of Jefferson Davis in a paper he presented to the Mises Institute in 1995 titled "The Secession Tradition in America." The student wondered if Livingston's statement, "Jefferson Davis was an enlightened slave holder who said that once the Confederacy gained its independence, it would mean the end of slavery. The Confederate Cabinet agreed to abolish slavery within five years after the cessation of hostilities in exchange for recognition by Britain and France," was factually accurate.

Jefferson Davis was, as Livingston suggests, an "enlightened slaveholder." He was well known as a kind master, even going as far as establishing a trial system on his plantation in Mississippi for punishment rather than resorting to the lash. He was not considered an ardent pro-slavery ideologue or a vehement "fire-eater" during the secession crisis in the months leading to war in 1861. As a member of the famous Committee of 13 charged with sorting through various compromise proposals in 1860, Davis suggested a policy of dual majorities for any proposal to pass. He supported the Crittenden Compromise, which would have preserved slavery in the South as well as extended the Missouri Compromise line to the Pacific, but when Republicans on the Committee refused to support any compromise efforts, Davis voted against them. He wanted a compromise that was truly "national" in scope. Republicans chose Party over Union before, during, and after the War.

In 1864, Duncan F. Kenner, perhaps the largest slave holder in the South at the time and representative from Louisiana, approached Davis with a unique proposal. In order to gain the recognition of the British and French governments, something that had eluded the Confederacy since the beginning of the War, Kenner suggested that Davis tell both governments that the Confederacy would abolish slavery. No timeframe was discussed, and Kenner originally floated the idea of presenting the plan to the Confederate Congress. Davis asked Kenner not to do so and rejected the idea outright, thinking that the situation was not yet desperate enough to warrant such a move, but in late 1864 he sent for Kenner and told him to put the plan in motion. Kenner was given credentials and set out on a secret mission to Europe in January 1865. He arrived just weeks before Robert E. Lee surrendered at Appomattox Courthouse and met with the two Confederate commissioners, James M. Mason (grandson of George Mason) and John Slidell, in Paris. Slidell at first refused to support the plan, but Kenner told him that such refusal would result in his immediate suspension.

The three men met with French Emperor Napoleon III, who agreed to recognize the Confederacy under these terms if the British would follow suit. The commissioners quickly sailed to London, where they met with the Prime Minister, Henry John Temple, who sternly rebuked their proposal, stating that Her Majesty's government would never recognize the Confederacy under any condition. Lee's surrender dashed any lingering hopes of continuing diplomacy, and this last-ditch effort to win international support died a swift death.

Davis would have needed approval from his Cabinet to send such a mission, and Kenner's other task relating to a proposed joint British-Confederate bank with cotton used as operating capital certainly would have had input from the Confederate Secretary of the Treasury, George Trenholm, and Secretary of State, Judah P. Benjamin. Yet, such a plan would have required a commitment from the Southern states and a constitutional amendment, something they did not yet have but perhaps could have obtained if independence was secured.

Kenner's tale was recorded in 1899 by the historian William Wirt Henry, grandson of Patrick Henry, and is legitimate. The Library of Congress admitted its validity in 1916, and referenced the Joseph Brent Papers, now housed at Louisiana State University, as evidence. Brent married Kenner's daughter after the War, so he would have had conclusive proof.

The Slaveholders' Dilemma

WHEN I WAS IN GRADUATE SCHOOL in the 1990s, one of my professors assigned Eugene Genovese's *The Slaveholders' Dilemma* as part of our reading seminar on American history.

This was Genovese's first book in nearly a decade, and it marked a transition in his worldview. Genovese rose to prominence in the American historical profession in the late 1960s with the publication of *The Political Economy of Slavery*. He was a card carrying Marxist then, a young New Yorker wrapped in the Civil Rights Movement and the sixties laser focus on the "evil" South.

He followed up with *Roll, Jordan, Roll* in the mid-1970s, and even then, one could see a slight transition in Genovese's view of the South.

He admired the Southern people and thought Southern intellectuals should be taken seriously. These were not backwoods hicks who spent their days whittling and beating slaves. Nor were they lazy dimwits who drank bourbon and dueled over minor insults. Those things happened, certainly, but Genovese began to see the South and her people in a different light.

He never argued Southerners did not hold racial views that would make modern Americans blush. Nor did he refuse to remind Americans of the horrors of domestic slavery when they could be found.

But he also began to understand just how important the South and the Southern tradition was to America. He dedicated *The Slaveholders' Dilemma* to Clyde Wilson, M.E. Bradford, and John Shelton Reed, three of the most important Southern intellectuals of the last quarter of the twentieth century.

Genovese had also abandoned his love affair with Karl Marx and returned to his native Catholicism in 1996.

His work over the next twenty years exposed the deep complexities of the Southern tradition. Rather than a pre-modern feudal society, the South, in Genovese's estimation, was a progressive world that attempted to resist the worst elements of middle class "progress" while embracing the best of what America had to offer.

This is what made the South great and why Genovese argued that Americans could learn from men like St. George Tucker, John Taylor of Caroline and John C. Calhoun along with the agrarians of *I'll Take My Stand*.

He said as much in *The Slaveholders' Dilemma*. My only exposure to Genovese before being assigned this book was through his earlier Marxist infused writings. I was surprised to see Clyde Wilson's name in the front of the book and expressed that to my professor.

He smiled and said, "Why do you think he dedicated that book to Clyde?" I had no answer because I didn't know of Genovese's conversion.

But the introduction to *The Slaveholders' Dilemma* stuck, and as such became an important part of how I thought about the South.

Twitter Historians Distort History, Again

MARJORIE TAYLOR GREENE forced the political left into an apoplectic rage two weeks ago when they discovered she intended to form an "America First Caucus" based on "Anglo-Saxon political traditions." Clearly, this showed that Representative Greene intended to force "white supremacy" on the rest of the United States. After all, she openly displayed her racism by using the term "Anglo-Saxon." Only racists—i.e. Southerners, former Confederates, Klansmen, anti-immigrationists and the like—used that term to describe "white supremacist" immigration and political policies in the nineteenth and early twentieth centuries. This leftist two-minutes of hate mirrored the outrage over then Attorney General Jeff Sessions's claim that the legal system in the United States is based on "Anglo-American" traditions, a phrase that has been widely and correctly used for over a century to define the American political and legal order. Greene is largely too inexperienced and dense to understand the difference between "Anglo-Saxon" and "Anglo-American," but this was probably her intended meaning.

Regardless, Twitter historians immediately jumped into action to support this new woke crusade against language and more importantly provide evidentiary cover for the claim that "Anglo-Saxon" has been nothing more than another term for "white supremacy." Lead Twitter historian Kevin Kruse penned a piece for MSNBC linking early twentieth-century "Anglo-Saxon" rhetoric to the rise of Nazi Germany. Kevin Levin, a Boston based "freelance teacher" who has become a darling of the Twitter historian brigade for his attacks on the "Lost Cause," produced a Twitter thread with several examples of Confederate monuments and dedication speeches that in his mind used the term "Anglo-Saxon" as a code for "white supremacy."

Did racists used the term "Anglo-Saxon" in white supremacist speeches in the nineteenth and early twentieth centuries? Yes. But as Kruse illustrates, this language found favor among most Americans, meaning that America, North and South, was racist at the turn of the century. This isn't news. Anyone who has read American history knows that Americans a century or more ago held racial views at odds with modern American society. Did some Southerners use the term to describe racial hegemony in the South? Yes, but this does not mean Confederate monuments or other symbols were built to maintain "white supremacy." That was already a given in the post-Reconstruction period. This also presents several questions: First, did these racialists intend "Anglo-Saxon" to mean all white people or a racial subgroup of Europeans? Second, what did "Anglo-Saxon traditions" mean to the men who used the term? And third, was the term only used by "white supremacists" to defend the racial order in the United States, or was this a description of a larger legal and political tradition adapted to a variety of circumstances?

The term "Anglo-Saxon" was widely used in the middle of the nineteenth century to differentiate Americans of English stock from those of Ireland or other European nations. Abraham Lincoln made this clear in his famous 1858 rebuttal of Stephen Douglas at Freeport in 1858 when he suggested that the founding generation did not intend the Declaration of Independence to apply only to "rich men" or "white men" or "Anglo-Saxon white men" but to all men. Lincoln was a white supremacist, but his use of the term "Anglo-Saxon" did not connote any hint of a racial order in 1858. In the twentieth century, Theodore Roosevelt chaffed at suggestions that he was an "Anglo-Saxon." During a 1902 speech, he said, "I haven't got any English blood in me. Someone once introduced me as a typical specimen of the Anglo-Saxon. I was glad for once to find what Anglo-Saxon was, because I was half Dutch and half Irish." The famous Southern journalist Irvin S. Cobb explained to a New York audience in 1917 that many of the Southerners who had been classified as "Anglo-Saxon" were in fact Celtic and could not be considered "Anglo-Saxon" in any form. To Lincoln, Roosevelt, and Cobb, Anglo-Saxon carried a distinctly English meaning and was not intended as a broad term for "white Americans." Kruse admits as much in his piece. Anti-immigration proponents who warned against large scale immigration in the 1920s were focusing almost entirely on Eastern Europeans in their diatribes, meaning other white people. If "Anglo-Saxon" was a code word for "white supremacy," it undoubtedly ignored large sections of Europe.

Levin's contention that "Anglo-Saxon traditions" served as a code word for "white supremacy" would mean that large groups of *Northerners* would also be guilty of the sin, including many men who used the term during ceremonies dedicated to *Union* veterans, Northern events, and Northern leaders.

Poet George William Bell wrote in 1913 that "Lincoln's Anglo-Saxon blood runs pure throughout its English, Northern, Southern course...." Others described Lincoln's language as "pure Anglo-Saxon." A British politico mourned Lincoln's assassination in May 1865 with the hope that "the great Norman Anglo-Saxon family in all its branches throughout both hemispheres, all sprung from the same race, may hereafter live in brotherly union and love, contributing to the happiness and welfare of each and all, and giving to the world a bright example of concord, progress, and civilization." At a 1909 centurial tribute to Lincoln in Chicago, several speakers used the term "Anglo-Saxon liberty" and "Anglo-Saxon democracy" to describe the triumph of the *Union* during the War. Does this make Lincoln, his legacy, and his monuments symbols of "white supremacy"? If you follow Levin's logic, then yes.

The term Anglo-Saxon was applied to a host of other Union men as well. At a dedication ceremony for a statue to Ulysses S. Grant at Fairmont Park in Philadelphia, one speaker to "great applause" said that North America was saved for the "Anglo-Saxon" and that Grant melded this "brotherhood" together in an indestructible Union, evidently of white supremacists.

At the 1914 dedication of monuments to Union Generals Meade, Hancock and Reynolds at Gettysburg, one speaker remarked that Confederate soldiers were "bone of our bone, flesh of our flesh, and Anglo-Saxons," meaning, according to Levin, that all Civil War soldiers, but particularly these three generals, were white supremacists.

Republican Indiana war governor Oliver P. Morton was described as the unveiling of his monument in Indianapolis as a man of tremendous "Anglo-Saxon strength," a clear dog whistle that Indiana needed to maintain "white supremacy."

People in New England and Canada dedicated monuments to eighteenth century wars near the close of the nineteenth century. The President of the Bunker Hill Monument Association remarked in 1896 that "many of our privileges came down as heirlooms from the Anglo-Saxon race...."

The Bennington, Vermont Battle Monument dedication ceremony in 1891, attended by President Benjamin Harrison, featured an address which argued that Americans were "more true to their birthright of Anglo-Saxon freedom and liberty" than British citizens. Levin would certainly think this meant these people favored white supremacist government and that President Harrison was, by default, a white supremacist for attending the event.

A Massachusetts speaker remarked at the Lousibourg, Cape Breton, Canada memorial dedication in 1895—erected as an "inspiration to heroism of for all generations of Anglo-Saxons," in a region dominated by people of French descent—that, "We are for the most part Anglo-Saxons today, and we are here to recognize and to glorify certain qualities which characterize that race." Obviously, this monument to "Anglo-Saxon" white supremacy needs to be removed.

At the 1891 dedication ceremony for the Candia, New Hampshire Soldiers Monument—which honored fallen Candia men in three American wars—the Reverend Samuel C. Beane said, "From that day to this, there have been, by people of Anglo-Saxon blood and their allies, four memorable contests for the destruction of arbitrary power and the restoration of men to their natural rights." This included the "Civil War," a contest that he argued began only out of a struggle of patriotism to "regain a few forts and save the national territory from dismemberment" that eventually transformed into a crusade to erase "every line of color and race that subjected man to man." To Beane, this was part of the "Anglo-Saxon tradition," but how could this be so? Surely Beane should have anticipated that twenty-first century woke leftists would think that references to "Anglo-Saxon" were made only to support "white supremacy."

Most Americans in the nineteenth and early twentieth centuries, North and South, understood the phrase "Anglo-Saxon traditions" and "Anglo-Saxon civilization" to mean self-government, heroism, individual liberty, and the rule of law. As Beane contended, these principles were handed down through generations of Englishmen beginning at Runnymede in 1215 and later transported to American shores. That Americans of all ethnic backgrounds referenced it, North and South, in a variety of contexts should provide a clue to woke Twitter historians that language should be analyzed within the context of the period, not from twenty-first century presentism.

By and large all Americans wanted to maintain a traditional "Anglo-Saxon civilization" one hundred years ago, but this meant a heritage linked to the old world and defined by traditional political institutions, not a racial order or "white supremacy," even during the height of the "Lost Cause." As the historian Charles Reagan Wilson wrote in his *Baptized in Blood*, "Race was intimately related to the story of the Lost Cause but was not the basis of it, and was not the center of it."

In fact, memorials and dedication ceremonies were never intended to be political events and had no political meaning. The historian Gaines Foster argued in his *Ghosts of the Confederacy* that most Southerners paid little attention to the dedication speeches and that these events were *intended* to be apolitical. "More important, by placing the celebration of Memorial Day under the charge of women and hence within the realm of sentiment, southerners further reduced any political or ideological implications. That some blacks, even ones active in politics, could contribute to the memorial work also indicated how little political content it had."

In other words, Twitter historians like Levin should be embarrassed to post most of their nonsense, but that would require a level of self-awareness and honesty they frankly lack. Unfortunately, their polemics often pass for "scholarship" in the modern academy, a result of the transformation of the profession from real critical thinking and understanding to a thinly-veiled propaganda arm of the modern woke movement.

"Daniel Boone Was A Man"

"DANIEL BOONE WAS A MAN, yes a big man." So began the (now not so) famous Ballad of Daniel Boone by legendary Southern actor Fess Parker. Parker portrayed Boone from 1964-1970 on the television series of the same name. It would be impossible to produce that show today. Boone is the antithesis of the modern American man. He hunted. He was an honest, rugged individual, and more importantly a Southerner. He was manly in the way Jefferson described the word in the Declaration of Independence. He was frugal and though it ruined him financially, repaid his debts. He fought American Indians (though he treated them with respect). He served with distinction in the American War for Independence with George Rogers Clark. Such actions don't make a hero in America any longer. American men are now defined by "Pajama Boy."

This wasn't always the case. Americans, both North and South, considered Boone to be the quintessential American man. So did Europeans. Thomas Cole, the founder of the Hudson River School of art, dedicated a canvas to him in 1826. Boone was the inspiration for the character Natty Bumpoo (Hawkeye) in James Fenimore Cooper's *Letherstocking Tales*. The famous romantic poet Lord Byron made Boone a character in his *Don Juan*. Southern naturalist John James Audubon went hunting with Boone in Kentucky and later sketched a portrait. Audubon was amazed at Boone's skill as a hunter and described him as "a stout, hale, and athletic man, dressed in a homespun hunting shirt, bare-legged and moccasined, carried a long and heavy rifle, which, as he was loading it, he said had proved efficient in all his former undertakings, and which he hoped would not fail on this occasion, as he felt proud to show me his skill." He then blew up a squirrel. PETA probably wants that phrase struck from Audubon's account.

Part III: Southern Comfort

Boone not only defined the American man, he defined the American spirit, a spirit that was forged by his experiences in the South and the Southern frontier. He always thought of himself as a common American. This is true. The common man in early American history did many extraordinary things. They didn't wait around for someone to bail them out, blaze trails, or achieve success. Nothing was given to them and they expected nothing less. These were rugged, tough individuals with Southerners setting the standard. By erasing this part of our history, and in particular Southern history, we destroy what made America great. Sadly, that has always been the objective, I think.

Sunnyside and Sleepy Hollow

APRIL 3 WAS WASHINGTON Irving's birthday. While not a Southerner, Irving would have supported the South in its fight for independence in 1861 had he been alive to see it. He at least would have been opposed to coercion. Many notable New Yorkers, and for that matter Canadians, too, believed the same. Two fine treatments on this issue are Clint Johnson's *A Vast and Fiendish Plot* and Adam Mayers's *Dixie and the Dominion*.

Irving spent a considerable portion of his adult life in Europe. As with Southerner James Johnston Pettigrew, he was attracted to Spanish culture and enjoyed European aristocratic life, which he believed had many similarities with traditional American culture. Irving's estate, Sunnyside (pictured above), is a beautiful villa inspired by European architecture. Leading Southerners would have felt quite at home there. Irving considered the estate to be more than a home. He was tied to its soul.

Iriving's work often showed a disdain for the American bourgeoisie and most importantly self-righteous Yankee superiority. Ichabod Crane exemplified this attitude. Crane was a deluded buffoon, a money-grubber, and believed himself to be the intellectual master of the unenlightened souls of Sleepy Hollow, New York. Crane was from Connecticut. The real New Yorkers ran him out of town. Irving also wrote a multi-volume biography of George Washington which was considered to be the best treatment of the quintessential American hero for many decades.

He had contact with most of the leading members of American society during his life. He was friends with Dolly Madison and counted several presidents among his associates. His description of Washington, D.C.–and both James and Dolly Madison–during Madison's presidency is illuminating:

> I emerged from dirt and darkness into the blazing splendor of Mrs. Madison's drawing-room. Here I was most graciously received; found a crowded collection of great and little men, of ugly old women and beautiful young ones, and in ten minutes was hand and glove with half the people in the assemblage. Mrs. Madison is a fine, portly, buxom dame, who has a smile and a pleasant word for everybody. Her sisters, Mrs. Cutts and Mrs. Washington, are like two merry wives of Windsor; but as to Jemmy Madison,—oh, poor Jemmy! —he is but a withered little apple-john.

Irving described Baltimore society as so inviting one could get lost and never return. He tried to avoid it for that reason. It must be noted that Irving was a typical Northerner during much of the antebellum period. He recognized the value in Southern culture and considered Southerners to be of kindred spirit. Much changed in the ensuing decades.

Calhoun's Definition of Conservative

ONCE UPON A TIME, in a galaxy far, far away, Yankees could praise Calhoun and everyone cheered. This was normal.

In 1910, the Massachusetts born and bred Henry Cabot Lodge gave a gallant speech on the Senate floor praising John C. Calhoun as one of the truly great Americans in its history. This was to honor the placement of Calhoun's statue in Statuary Hall at the United States Capitol.

He said, "But Calhoun was much more even than this. He was one of the most remarkable men, one of the greatest minds that American public life can show. It matters not that before the last tribunal the verdict went against him, that the extreme doctrines to which his imperious logic carried him have been banned and barred, the man remains greatly placed in our history. The unyielding courage, the splendid intellect, the long devotion to the public service, the pure, unspotted private life are all there, are all here with us now, untouched and unimpaired for after ages to admire."

Imagine a Yankee saying this today. Better yet, imagine just about *anyone* in Congress saying this today.

The only way you can mention Calhoun in public today is with a firm denunciation followed by genuflecting to Abraham Lincoln. And sometimes that isn't even enough.

We live in a time of pure stupidity.

I had the honor of working with the greatest Calhoun scholar in the world in graduate school, Clyde Wilson.

If you were to ask him to point to an important Calhoun speech, he would often reference Calhoun's remarks on the admission of Michigan as a States in 1837.

Why? Because Calhoun defines the meaning of American conservatism in this speech. He also outlines the proper understanding of American sovereignty.

Calhoun said:

> because I am a conservative I am a State's rights man. I believe that in the rights of the States are to be found the only effectual means of checking the overaction of this Government; to resist its tendency to concentrate all power here, and to prevent a departure from the constitution; or, in case of one, to restore the Government to its original simplicity and purity. State interposition, or, to express it more fully, the right of a State to interpose her sovereign voice as one of the parties to our constitutional compact, against the encroachments of this Government, is the only means of sufficient potency to effect all this….As a conservative and a State's rights man, or if you will have it, a nullifier, I have, and shall resist all encroachments on the constitution, whether it be the encroachment of this Government on the States, or the opposite; the Executive on Congress, or Congress on the Executive. My creed is to hold both Governments, and the departments of each to their proper sphere, and to maintain the authority of the laws and the constitution against all revolutionary movements.

This is one of his most substantial public statements. First, it's not tied in any way to "defending slavery." Calhoun was insisting that Michigan be admitted to the Union by the will of her people and not by some demand from Congress. Second, Calhoun understood that the federal republic could only be maintained if the people of the States could check unconstitutional edicts from the general government. And third, Calhoun expanded nullification to include checks and balances in every level of government. This was not simply a State vs. Federal issue.

Conservative as "Defender of Liberty"

IN 1960, THE GREAT SOUTHERN political philosopher Richard Weaver penned an essay titled "Conservatism and Libertarianism: The Common Ground."

Most people considered Weaver to be a "conservative," and he accepted the term, but he also thought American conservatives and libertarians had much in common and should work together for a common goal: liberty.

The current internal warfare in both conservative and libertarian camps makes this essay relevant.

Weaver would not have found much in common with modern neoconservatives nor would he agree with left libertarians. The "conservatives" and "libertarians" in Weaver's essay are the so-called "paleoconservatives" and the Right Libertarians like Murray Rothbard, Ron Paul, Lew Rockwell, and others.

And indeed, both of these groups do have much in common, as Weaver illustrated in this beautiful essay.

Weaver defined a "conservative" as "a realist, who believes that there is a structure of reality independent of his own will and desire." That reality is determined by "a creation which was here before him" and that will exist long after he is gone, a reality that is regulated by human experience and independent of the individual and while not hostile to the individual "cannot be changed radically and arbitrarily." Most important, "man cannot make his will his law."

This is precisely the goal of the left, the reformer, the progressive, and Weaver–in 1960–warned against a particular type of radical, one who would "get control of the state to make all men equal or to make all men rich, or failing that to make all men equally unhappy." The state then becomes the instrument to drive the rest of America to radical's Utopian dream, or for the conservative and libertarian, a dystopian nightmare. In Weaver's estimation, this is where the traditional American had to make his stand.

To Weaver, this is the hill on which conservatives and libertarians could form their bulwarks, for the glue that held them together in 1960, and still does to this day, at least the paleos on both sides, was John C. Calhoun's understanding of the Constitution as a "negative document."

Weaver pegged that understanding to Calhoun, but the Southern tradition is built on this legal understanding. John Taylor, St. George Tucker, John Randolph, Abel Upshur and every Old Republican who warred Hamilton's constitutional machinations insisted that the ratifiers of the Constitution sold the document as a limited grant of power restricted by the Bill of Rights and the acknowledgment that all powers not expressly given were reserved to the States and the people thereof.

No one can read the public ratification debates without coming to this conclusion.

Weaver buttressed his claim of conservative and libertarian solidarity by arguing that both sides agreed in a natural "order of things which will largely take care of itself if you leave it alone." Government "corrections" of political "problems" would typically result in an unending progression of more costly and dangerous situations. Government cannot fix nature, but this has been the dream of every progressive since Marx scribbled his *Communist Manifesto*.

He also warned against the disposition of the modern radical to silence dissent and prophesied Big Tech's war on the modern right:

> It requires only a little experience in politics or publishing for one to learn that the enemies of freedom today are the radicals and the militant liberals. Not only do they propose through their reforms to reconstruct and regiment us, they also propose to keep us from hearing the other side. Anyone who has contended with Marxists and their first cousins, the totalitarian liberals, knows that they have no intention of giving the conservative alternative a chance to compete with their doctrines for popular acceptance. If by some accident they are compelled to physically listen, it is with indifference or a contempt because they really consider the matter a closed question–that is, no longer on the agenda of discussable things.

Weaver summarized that his "instincts are libertarian" and claimed that he "never would have joined with the conservatives if [he] had not been convinced that they are the defenders of freedom today." Notice he is not talking about

Lincoln's Grand Old Party but "conservatives." He considered conservatives to be the "tolerant" and "humane" man because he "didn't feel that terrible need to exterminate the enemy...." For the American, George Washington exemplified the best of the conservative tradition, a "revolutionary" who sought not to overthrow but to maintain natural order and the rights of Englishmen."

Weaver suggested that the conservative–and his libertarian allies–were the proper defenders of liberty because they understood natural order, tolerated "diversity of life," and condemned arbitrary power, because as Blake wrote, "One law for the lion and the ox is oppression."

Catalonia and the Southern Tradition

CATALONIA HAS VOTED TO SECEDE from Spain. This is a remarkable development in modern Western civilization, particularly in the age of the modern bureaucratic unitary imperial State. It signals that not all Europeans agree with the borderless European Union pushed by the political class and that culture and true nationalism still mean something. The shocking Paris attacks this past weekend put an exclamation point on that belief. Catalonia is more French than Spanish and only part of Spain because of dynastic happenstances in the early modern period. The Catalonian people are seeking to preserve their cultural identity in a world that is quickly becoming less regionally identifiable, at least in the West. They see the only solution is separation from the cancer.

Predictably, the Spanish government has called the vote illegal and there are several large roadblocks to Catalonian independence, but the idea that the modern State with is vast resources and nightmarish bureaucracy is better at protecting life, liberty, property, and most importantly "happiness" is under siege in Europe, and justifiably so. Europe is being invaded and the people—at least a vocal remnant of true Western civilization—are reacting.

The same cannot be said for the United States. President Obama's briefing after the Paris attacks highlighted "universal values" of all of "humanity." This is a subtle though striking slap at Western civilization. There are no "universal values" nor any values of humanity. Not all cultures share the same beliefs, customs, traditions, or "values," at least not traditional Western values. While Europeans are engaging in a retrenchment of what made "happiness" possible in a civilized society, it seems most Americans are continuing to abandon those values in a continual rush for the newest consumer craze. Tradition does not mesh with expensive gadgets and trifling over $4 coffee cups.

The counterweight has long been the Southern tradition, both politically and culturally. It is the last vestige of American conservatism. This is why it was no shock to see two hit pieces on the traditional South appear in the same week.

The first from Townhall.com columnist Joshua Holdenried contended that altering the Mississippi State flag or simply removing it until it is changed would be the "conservative" approach to take. The other was an overt assault on the modern American "Tenth Amendment" movement in the *USA Today* under the title, "Secrecy, corruption and conflicts of interest pervade state governments." This piece concluded, "The results may be deflating to the two-thirds of Americans who, according to a recent poll, look to the states for policy solutions as gridlock and partisanship has overtaken Washington."

Holdenried is advancing the neoconservative approach to American politics, and even invokes Robert E. Lee, Edmund Burke, Russell Kirk, and G.K. Chesterton to defend his position. To Holdenried, the Mississippi State flag is neither conservative nor traditional, and because the flag would be changed through a democratic process, the people of Mississippi should embrace the result and accept the decision as Lee would have supposedly done. But he misses the point. The State flag *does* represent the Southern tradition, namely the legacy of 1776, American self-government, true American federalism, and the Christian agrarian order, a more substantial calling than simply a defense of race and slavery. The "battle flag" is the one lasting symbol of the conservative South and if it is removed, that South suffers another blow, even if the fist that delivers it is through majority plebiscite in Mississippi or an act of the legislature in South Carolina.

The *USA Today* piece fails to recognize *why* Americans are rushing to support State power. It is not because they fundamentally believe that State governments are Utopian systems of efficient administration; it is because their *culture* and *traditions* are under attack from an alien people, namely outsiders—even Americans from other States and regions—who do not share their values. The modern "State's rights" movement is a recognition that even in the United States there are no "universal values" and that the "pursuit of happiness" is being destroyed by aggressive and unconstitutional federal power. Many State governments are corrupt, but can anyone with a bit of integrity declare that the federal Leviathan is *less* corrupt or that the political class in Washington D.C. has any shred of integrity?

The Southern tradition is under assault because it represents the last vestige of opposition to the modern American empire, both foreign and domestic. The South retained the Jeffersonian promise that when governments failed to protect the life, liberty, and property of the people, it was their right to alter or to abolish that government and to institute a new government that protected their "safety and happiness." This tradition is worth exploring and defending, and Southerners should not let outside forces hijack and debase their history and society.

Alas, Southern symbols will continue to fall, because while Catalonia is rallying around a common heritage and culture, Southerners are rushing to abandon theirs. The nobles of France did the same thing in the early stages of the French Revolution, believing that appeasement would result in a more stable society and would allow them to maintain power. The bloody streets of Paris told another story. That should serve as sufficient evidence that the opposition will never relent until the old order, tradition, is eradicated by any means necessary.

Pope Francis and the Southern Tradition

RECENT ATTEMPTS MADE BY THE LEFT and the right to make Pope Francis one of "their" own has sparked considerable debate among the political class and their voices in the mainstream media. Pope Francis's speech before Congress was nothing more than a continuation of themes he has publicly endorsed throughout his time as pontiff, namely support for the environment and opposition to the excesses of capitalism, among others. He has been labeled a Marxist, and because the Latin American Catholic Church has flirted with political socialism for years, there is fear among both conservative Catholics and Protestants in the United States that the Pope's brand of Christianity is a thinly veiled design to bring Marxist political changes to America.

Do they have a point? To an extent.

Pope Francis made a mistake in addressing Congress. By standing before a secular body and urging political action from a group ill equipped to govern 30 people let alone 300 million, the Pope opened his call for reform to misguided attack. The changes he seeks are cultural, not political, and need to be made in the heart, not through legislation or regulation. That said, contrary to what political pundits on both sides have said, Pope Francis is neither "liberal" nor "conservative." He is a traditionalist, an advocate for traditional Christian charity and living, what Erasmus called "the philosophy of Christ."

The South was, and still is, the one region of the United States that has zealously clung to this tradition. Pope Francis could be classified as a Jeffersonian, and traditional Southern conservatives, now purged from acceptable public debate, echoed his sentiments long before the Pope rattled nerves in Washington D.C.

Take for example his position on the environment. Pope Francis has called for good stewardship of natural resources and a willingness to live with, not against, nature. Southerners have advanced this position since the first Englishmen planted their feet on American soil in the sixteenth century. This has held true into the modern age. The great Southern conservative philosopher Richard Weaver once wrote that:

> "The Southerner tends to look upon nature as something that is given and something that is finally inscrutable. This is equivalent to saying that he looks upon it as the creation of a creator. To some extent nature has to be used, but what man should seek in regard to nature is not a complete dominion but a modus vivindi, that is a manner of living together or a coming to terms with something that was here before our time and something that will be here after it."

John Taylor of Caroline, the Fugitive Agrarians, and Wendell Berry of Kentucky all have sought the same arrangement. Self-sustaining small farms and rural living were hallmarks of Southern society. It was not long ago that Weaver was championed by the mainstream conservative movement, but his views are now arcane and unfashionable to the self-anointed conservative "philosophers" in America.

Even today Callaway Gardens, the beautiful private nature reserve in Pine Mountain, Georgia, is a testament to managed conservation. Founded by the Callaway family in an effort to provide a natural sanctuary on once worn-out farmland, the Gardens balance nature and development in a way no government park or agency has been able to accomplish. The Pope's call for more government involvement in environmental projects is imprudent, but this does not minimize the tradition it supports, one that has shaped by the South in America for nearly four hundred years.

Pope Francis's attacks on capitalism also harken to those leveled by Southerners both before and after the War. The Jeffersonians favored free markets, but they shuddered at the evils of industrialization, namely the horrid working conditions of the "wage-slaves" of the North, which included a poor diet, poor living conditions, and a repressive often inhumane working environment. These critiques were, of course, often stimulated by attacks on the South's own labor system, but this does not diminish the validity of the barbs thrown at their Northern neighbors. The populists of the Tom Watson stripe attacked industrialization for the same reason. It was the independence of the worker and the value of the man in an agrarian life that called the Fugitives to push for the maintenance of an agricultural society.

Some Southern industrialists sought to mitigate those conditions when possible in the post bellum period. By the early twentieth century, Southern industrialist Fuller Callaway was revolutionizing the way people worked in Southern cotton mills. His motto: "If you are working with cows, you have to think like cow. If you are working with men, you have to think like them. And you must never expect them to do anything that isn't human."

Even into the late twentieth century, Southerners were setting the standard for a comfortable work environment. Bill Turner of the W.C. Bradley, Co. in Columbus, GA pioneered the field of "servant leadership." The Bradley Company at one time owned Coca-Cola, and still owns Charbroil and Zebco, but it was its passion for a strong family based working environment that set it apart. One of its companies, TSYS, has been ranked as one of the best companies to work for in America. The same is true for Columbus based AFLAC. These companies have never lost sight of the Southern paternalistic tradition in labor. That tradition has at its core a Christian concern for the individual worker, his family, and his soul. In that type of working environment, money and profit are not the only measures of success. Southerners knew that community and people mattered as much as the bottom line. This is all Pope Francis has said about the "evils" of modern capitalism.

Finally, Pope Francis's request for Christian charity and compassion for the weak, sick, and poor has always found favor in the South. To this day, Southerners donate more time and money to charity than any other people in the United States. The conservative columnist Dan Smoot once wrote that during the Great Depression, Southerners would literally give a poor man—of any color—the shirt of his back. In fact, he said Southerners were more willing to do so for black Americans than white. This help was always accompanied by a smile and a hand up.

If America wants to reinvigorate a more civil, Christian society based on community and faith, it needs to look no farther than the South, a region that despite its reputation among Northern "elites" has continued to be the traditional light in American life. Or maybe Southerners will just keep that to themselves. It might be more fun to watch delusional, self-righteous Yankees squirm during a Christian lecture. After all, modern American culture is their creation.

www.ingramcontent.com/pod-product-compliance
Lightning Source LLC
Chambersburg PA
CBHW031435160426
43195CB00010BB/740